Don't Bite the Apple 'Til You Check for Worms

In *Don't Bite the Apple 'Til You Check for Worms,* Ken Abraham offers unique insights and biblical teaching for addressing the struggles that you face every day as a single Christian. You'll find relevant advice that is laced with compassion. The topics discussed here include:

- *creative dating*
- *building friendships with the opposite sex*
- *practicing sexual self-control*
- *recognizing God's choice for your husband or wife*
- *understanding the different types of love*
- *choosing to remain single*
- *dating non-Christians*
- *practicing sexual purity*
- *the importance of establishing and upholding spiritual standards*

Don't Bite the Apple 'Til You Check for Worms

will encourage those who have been discouraged by the "dating scene," present positive principles for enjoying life to those who desire to remain single, and give those who are waiting for the right person a practical plan for discerning God's will.

Don't Bite the Apple 'Til You Check for Worms

Ken Abraham

Power Books

Fleming H. Revell Company
Old Tappan, New Jersey

Unless otherwise identified, Scripture quotations in this volume are from the New American Standard Bible, © The Lockman Foundation 1960, 1962, 1963, 1968, 1971, 1972, 1973, 1975, 1977.

Scripture quotations identified KJV are from the King James Version of the Bible.

Scripture quotations identified NIV are from the HOLY BIBLE: NEW INTERNATIONAL VERSION, copyright © 1978 by the New York International Bible Society. Used by permission of Zondervan Bible Publishers.

Scripture quotations identified PHILLIPS are from THE NEW TESTAMENT IN MODERN ENGLISH, Revised Edition—J. B. Phillips, translator. Copyright © J. B. Phillips 1958, 1960, 1972. Used by permission of Macmillan Publishing Co., Inc.

Verses marked TLB are taken from *The Living Bible,* Copyright © 1971 by Tyndale House Publishers, Wheaton, Ill. Used by permission.

Library of Congress Cataloging in Publication Data

Abraham, Ken.
  Don't bite the apple 'til you check for worms.

  1. Love (Theology)   2. Sex—Religious aspects—
Christianity.   3. Marriage—Religious aspects—
Christianity.   4. Courtship—Religious aspects—
Christianity.   I. Title.
BV4639.A27   1985   241'.66   85-1729
ISBN 0-8007-5190-6

TO my co-worker, my lover, and
my best friend . . .
my wife, Angela

Contents

7

Contents

Introduction

This book will help you sort out your ideas about love, sex, singleness, and marriage. If you are single and trapped in the dating doldrums, this book offers you hope. If you are single and plan to stay that way, this book presents positive principles to help you live life to the fullest. If you are a single who desires to be married, waiting for the right person, these pages will explode the mysteries concerning the search for your mate, and will show you a practical plan for discerning God's will.

Who am I? Why am I writing this book? Why do I think *I* have the answers? I travel the country with the Watchmen, a contemporary Christian musical group, geared toward youth. I'm the drummer. But I'm also a preacher and teacher. In my ministry, I have the opportunity of speaking to young people where they're at in language they can understand, through a medium to which they can relate.

In my work, I have noticed that the source of many youth problems is a dating or marriage relationship that ought not have occurred in the first place. My mental briefcase is chock-full of case studies illustrating the pain, frustration, and sorrow that come from our culture's confusion about sex, and roles, and right and wrong.

Every week I meet dozens of people who are hurting because they have chosen poorly in their social lives. These individuals believed the sensual imagery surrounding them, and cast aside their morality, only to end up with V.D.; perhaps an abortion; often deep-seated guilt; physical or emotional devastation; or spiritual disintegration. I meet young adults whose lives have been shattered because they married the wrong person, or they couldn't find any-one to marry, or they married outside the will of God. These are people who have bitten the apple without checking for worms.

The principles I present here as "worm medicine" all have biblical foundations. Even those things that we might consider as "common sense" have been sifted through the stringent sieve of Scripture.

I wrote every page of this book before I was married, because I've noticed a curious phenomenon among many married authors. They seem to suffer a bit from amnesia. They forget what it was really like to be single and sixteen—or single and twenty-six.

What you read here is what it feels like "today" to be a single person, threatened by pressure to conform, or to be caught in the battle of sexual temptation with no apparent, acceptable outlet.

On the other hand, I can tell you that God's ways work! His principles can be discovered, studied, and followed. I have tested them in my own life, and watched them work in the lives of hundreds of young men and women I talk to each year.

They can work for you.

KEN ABRAHAM

Don't Bite the Apple 'Til You Check for Worms

Part I

Rough Sailing on *The Love Boat* (Dating and Other Diversions)

1

Cruising the
Lonely Seas

The rock band was blaring aboard the bow section of the huge cruise liner as we gently cut through the warm Atlantic waters. Fellow members of the Watchmen and I were returning from a nineteen-day concert tour of Nova Scotia, and the pulsating sounds of drums, synthesizers, and guitars beckoned to the musician in me like a powerful electromagnet drawing fragments of metal across the ship's deck. Absently, I drifted in the direction of the music, locating its source in an ornate ballroom. It was only late afternoon, but already the dance floor was crammed with drunken passengers, awkwardly attempting to move their bodies to the beat of the throbbing rhythm.

"Happy Hour," they called it. I didn't feel very happy. I was alone. I looked into a few faces. Everyone was laughing, but they didn't seem very happy either.

I was jarred out of my contemplation by a wobbly young woman, wearing high heels, a skirt that was slit to her thigh, and an unbuttoned blouse that was loosely tied in the front. When she bumped into me, she bounced backward. For a moment she teetered as though she were going to fall, but then maintained her balance, and swayed back my way.

"Thanks for slowin' me down!" she gurgled. "I was goin' too

fast." She brought her face close to mine, and I could smell the booze and perfume. "Hey! Do you want to dance? You kinda caught my step," she laughed.

"Oh . . . ah, no thanks," I answered, trying my best to sound cool and sophisticated.

"What's the matter? Don't you like me?" she asked.

I glanced around and thought people were watching us.

"No, no!" I assured her, hoping to calm her down. "I like you just fine. I'm not much of a dancer."

She swayed dangerously again and breathed disgustedly in my face. "Pervert!" she said loudly, and wobbled away.

Her outburst drew the gaze of nearly every person in the room. Funny thing, *I* felt embarrassed. I hastily made my exit from the "Happy Hour." Outside, I thought, *You can't win! If you try to hustle the girls, you're a playboy. If you don't pay any attention, you're a weirdo!*

I walked on down the corridor where dozens of people had congregated around the slot machines. At least seventy-five quarters fell into the one-armed bandits in the brief time span it took me to walk by. None yielded a return.

I opened the door to the stairwell and was stunned by the large sign hanging on the wall. I read: FREE X-RATED MOVIES, TONIGHT, 7:00 P.M.—SHIP'S THEATER.

What's a Christian to Do?

I continued down the stairwell, out another door, and onto one of the ship's sun decks. The sun had almost gone down, and the air felt slightly cool to my skin. I walked over to the railing of the ship, placed my elbows on the rail, and plopped my chin into my hands. For the next hour, I stayed that way, watching the wake of the ship follow us through the ocean.

I was feeling sorry for myself and upset with the Lord.

"God, do You know how tough it is to be a single Christian guy today? Why, it would be so easy to give in to all the temptations around here! I'm a thousand miles from home. Hardly anyone on the boat knows my name. Nobody would ever find out. It would be so easy . . . !"

No visions parted the skies. It seemed in that vast expanse of blue sky and blue water, God was nowhere to be found. Only the slushing of the water against the side of the boat broke the silence. I remembered a few Scriptures I'd been taught as a kid.

Ghosts of Scriptures Past

Most of them I knew by heart, but some I had never memorized or even thought about previously. Some of the verses caused me to be uncomfortable. "Do not be conformed to this world, but be transformed . . . ." "Come out from among them." "Be ye separate." "You shall be holy for I am holy."

One passage kept reoccurring:

Do not be bound together with unbelievers; for what partnership have righteousness and lawlessness, or what fellowship has light with darkness?

2 Corinthians 6:14

Don't Be Docked in the Wrong Port!

My ministry has borne out the truth of that verse. Fully 75 percent of my work with youth and single adults deals with cleaning up the mess in an unequally yoked relationship: like Christians dating non-Christians and winding up with a baby or an abortion; Christians marrying non-Christians and living a life of hellish coexistence, both partners citizens of different kingdoms; Christians marrying nonbelievers and ending their marriages in divorce, wondering what went wrong, when, in fact, the wedding should never have occurred.

You can avoid such a miserable marriage mishap if you will establish the proper patterns in your premarital social life. To help you do so, let's carefully examine that mysterious American folk ritual called *dating*.

2

The Rocks and Roles of Dating

Once upon a time, long ago, young people did not date. Their parents guided their social lives and romantic futures. Mom and Dad made the matrimonial arrangements, and the younger generation had to live with their parents' choices.

In the twentieth century, youth are more independent. They like to plot their own courses. (I remember getting ready for a date. The nervousness. The excitement. Meeting the girl. Would she like me? What would happen?) Probably every guy and girl has nervous or fearful reactions when anticipating a date, but if you know the right "roles" in dating before embarking upon your social adventures, you can avoid a lot of rocks along the way.

Viva la Différence!

Let's start with the basics. God has assigned specific roles to the male and female, and these roles are not the same. Notice in Genesis 1:27 it says, "Male and female he created them." *God did not create unisex!* He did not create *hes, shes,* and *shims!* A man has been given the responsibility to "lead" in the dating-mating relationship, while the woman's role is to be that of a "helpmate," one who inspires, encourages.

These roles have not been assigned because of any supposed superiority or inferiority of the sexes. God is not a male chauvinist. Men are not intrinsically more intelligent than women and, therefore, more deserving of the leadership responsibilities in a relationship. Neither are women less able to discern deep spiritual truths and, as such, required to look to their male counterpart for divine direction. The functions of men and women have nothing to do with our abilities or merit.

I don't pretend to understand it, but God's handiwork in nature shows that He is a God of order. He does not share with us His logic concerning this arrangement. He simply presents His plan and informs us that this is how male and female interact most meaningfully. The Bible depicts the man as the "head," the leader, while the woman should be the "heart," the life support. What's more important—to lead or to live? Neither! *Both* are necessary.

Here, then, is a marvelous and exciting concept: that male and female are wonderfully unique, equally important, yet designed by our Creator to be interdependent and complementary to each other. The roles God has ordained for men and women are not contradictory or contentious, when they are played out according to His Word. Rather, the roles are supplementary to each other, and make for the greatest possible degree of harmony. Order, when respected, can help make for good relationships—even good dating experiences.

It's a Man's Job

Men, your responsibility is to be the leader! How many times have you heard that, guys? One way you can demonstrate your leadership is by making the arrangements for the date and bearing the financial responsibility for it. (This is not to say that girls cannot occasionally ask a guy out, make the necessary arrangements, or pay for a date.) It may fly in the face of what we've been told by the Women's Liberation Movement, but I have found that most young women prefer the traditional pattern when it comes to the nitty-gritty business of asking someone out.

"I can't stand it when my boyfriend calls me up and asks, 'What do you want to do tonight?' " one young woman complained to me at a church meeting, after one of our concerts. "I would much rather he called me up with some idea about where he wants to go, and what he wants to do."

The Leading Man.   Far more important than the role a young man plays in the perfunctory details involved in the dating process is the spiritual leadership he brings to the relationship. If a couple is to function as God originally planned, the man must take his proper place as a spiritual leader. Paul writes: ". . . Christ is the head of every man, and the man is the head of a woman, and God is the head of Christ" (1 Corinthians 11:3). If the man shirks this responsibility, the relationship is headed down a rocky road.

I often recommend that couples pray before every date. You should see how people react to *that!* When I make the suggestion during a seminar, a rift of chuckles ripples through the audience. Even young Christian women cannot imagine their dates pausing for prayer, before pulling out of the driveway. After we talk about it for a while, most admit that such a practice would definitely set a different tone for their social lives. Nevertheless few young men or women are courageous enough to suggest such an idea to their dates. First dates, especially, are a problem, but even then it *is* the male's responsibility to lead!

It is the man's responsibility to see that everything that occurs during each date is honoring and pleasing to Christ.

Men, ask yourself a few honest questions: "Am I helping or hindering her spiritual life? Am I building her up as a Christian, or helping to tear her down? Is she a better or worse person in God's sight after having dated me?" If, through honest analysis, you discover that you have been a drag on your date's spiritual life, rather than an uplift to her, you should confess your shortcoming to Christ, ask His forgiveness, and then apologize to your date. Frankly admit to her that you were doing her an injustice by not being the spiritual leader and example that God wants you to be.

Then, pray together for your heavenly Father's help to rightly conduct your social lives in the future. Sound crazy? It works!

So, What's a Girl to Do?

I have asked many audiences around the country, "What do you
feel is the man's responsibility in a dating relationship?" First, of
course, we have some fun:

"Pay for the date," says one.

"Show me a good time," says another. Finally we get down to the
role of male leadership. However, when I ask questions concerning
the *woman's* responsibility or role in the dating relationship, the answers are much more ambiguous.

"It may sound silly," one attractive dental assistant told me, "but
I never realized that I should be taking an active part during a date.
I felt it was the guy's responsibility to entertain me, and it was my
job to give away as little of myself as possible in return for his kindness. That was selfish, but I honestly never dreamed that God made
any other demands of me while on a date, except to have fun and
keep my virginity."

In a midwestern city a teenage girl commented, "Well, I guess if
the guy's place is to lead, my place is to follow." That didn't win her
much applause, but it opened up discussions.

Another young woman raised a valid question: "I know the Bible
says the wife should submit to her husband, but Dan and I aren't
married yet. What should my role be?"

The ideas of following and submission do not sit very well with
twentieth-century women. The words immediately conjure up an
image of a woman who hangs around the house and comes running
like Lassie every time her man snaps his fingers. This is decidedly
not the biblical interpretation of a submissive woman. (Take a look
at the active, practical, wise woman of Proverbs 31.)

It seems to me that the role of a woman in a dating relationship is not to be subject to her date (whatever that might mean), but rather one who "inspires." It is no secret that with a little encouragement from their female companions, men have aspired to heights they might never have attained had they been left on their own. Down through the ages, great men in politics, religion, and nearly every other field have pointed to women in their lives who have spurred them on to success.

Potential for Influence. The Christian young woman must recognize the potential she has for influencing her date, either positively or negatively. *What do I want to inspire this man to do or to be?* she should ask herself. Now this doesn't mean that she can't aspire to great things herself. The spiritually mature young woman suggests by her behavior and example that her date is to be the man of God that the Lord desires him to be. The way she dresses, the things she says and does, should all be done in an attempt to inspire her date to walk more like and more closely to Jesus Christ.

While attending Asbury College, I dated a young woman who knew how to do this. In many subtle ways she inspired me to be a man of God. With a loving and gentle spirit she gently prodded and encouraged me to develop those characteristics that emulated Christ, while she helped me to avoid anything that did not glorify Jesus. As she influenced me to live closer to the Lord, I took the spiritual leadership responsibilities of our relationship and treated her as a deserving woman of God.

Women, if you will be sensitive to the opportunities that present themselves to encourage your date, the consideration will reap huge dividends. Watch carefully for chances to compliment those traits about your date that you would like to see him put forward in his personality or life-style. Before long, you will begin to notice those characteristics developing in him. Men can do the same.

"I never knew what a good time we could have," a young secretary exclaimed, "until I began looking for new ways to inspire my guy to be more like Christ! I used to think that my role was just to be the gushy, fawning type. When I began taking an active, constructive part in our relationship, looking for ways to point Jimmy toward Christ, dating took on a whole new meaning for me! Not that I try to turn our evenings out into church services. I'm just trying to make our social lives more interesting and uplifting."

This "Divine Right" Is Wrong

Young women often ask me, "How do I know if this guy's for me?" My answer is, if he will not accept the responsibility to be the spiritual leader in the relationship, then you can be relatively certain that he is not the man God has in mind to complete your life. By the same token, if a guy finds a young woman will not accept his leadership and insists upon playing the dominant role in the relationship, he should be wise enough to recognize that it's going to be hard for him to fulfill himself in that relationship.

What if the leader is inadequate? In order for a woman of God to submit to the leadership of the man of God, his leadership must be sound, practical, and most important of all, biblical. His guidance should show clear markings of spiritual depth and maturity *if* he expects her to follow his example and to profit from his leadership. *A girl should never marry a man whose spiritual leadership she cannot follow.*

Remember, a dating couple is not a married couple. The man does not have a "Divine Right" to rule on spiritual matters in a marriage, much less in a dating situation. She is not bound legally or scripturally to accept your leadership, young man, if it contradicts that which the Spirit of God has borne witness of to her. He can inspire or illuminate the heart and mind of a woman as easily as He can that of a man.

Jolene, a spiritually mature Christian, approached me after I had spoken at her church in Atlanta. "Bob is very demanding. He insists that I submit to his spiritual leadership," she sobbed, "but I'm convinced that he is wrong in his interpretation of the Scripture. I want him to be the spiritual leader of our relationship, but I can't go against what is right."

I had an opportunity to talk with Bob, and Jolene was right. He was equating a matter of personal conviction with a general biblical principle. Being a spiritual leader doesn't mean being a spiritual bully. It means living at its deepest level—like Christ.

3

Dating Is Building Friendships

What's the purpose of dating? Earlier, I mentioned that dating should be the "training ground" for marriage. Here, then, are a few other suggestions how you might best take advantage of your training days.

In dating, seek to build friendships rather than commitments. While it is true that commitment is a primary ingredient for love and marriage, many men and women try to force too much too soon. Let the commitments take place naturally or not at all. Besides, the best lovers are best friends.

Norah Lee Allen, wife of the Oak Ridge Boys' Duane Allen, once told me, "Ken, I married my best friend! Before we were engaged, Duane and I shared our deepest joys and sorrows. He was the one I went to when I needed help. Now that we are married, we have so much to talk about. I'm glad our love grew out of our friendship, rather than the other way around."

At many schools, if you date the same person twice, or are seen talking in the hallway, you are practically committed for life. Much the same is true in the business office or factory. Consequently, you must take special steps to avoid these superficial ties that oftentimes constrain you against your will. The best remedy I know is to try making *friends* rather than lovers out of your dates.

Getting to Know You

A guy I know makes a point of trying to learn as much as he can about the girls he dates. If he has dated the same girl in the past, he makes a conscious effort to learn at least one new thing about her each time he is with her—her interests, hobbies, dreams, and goals; at the same time, he tries to share at least one meaningful part of his life with every girl he dates. He's not being nosy. He isn't pushy. He honestly tries to establish deep and lasting friendships, and that's just plain smart! My friend is not an overly handsome fellow, nor is he an excessive spender on his dates—yet he is extremely popular. Why? Because he has learned how to make a friend and to be a friend of his date.

Talking: The Main Course

If you are going to truly seek to get to know a person—talk to him or her. But just think of how many dates involve *non*talking activities: movies, concerts, football games, and so forth. It is virtually impossible to learn about a person on a deep intellectual, emotional, or spiritual level, if you spend all your time as a spectator. Kissing, hugging, and petting can also be forms of intimate *non*-communication. If you really want to get to know the person you are with—*talk!*

"Oh, yuk!" one teenage girl blurted out loud, when I shared this with her church youth group. "You've got to be kidding!" She continued, "Nobody wants to just *talk* on a date anymore."

"What are *you* looking for in a date?" I asked. (She blushed.) "If you are just dating to relieve some of your sexual energy, that's one thing. But, if you are sincerely looking for a meaningful, and perhaps lasting, relationship, that's another."

Then I told this story: "Once when I was dating a girl, I took her to a drive-in. As the movie progressed, so did we. Beginning at first with a casual kiss, we moved to more prolonged, involved embracing. Suddenly, in the middle of a kiss, she pulled away."

"You don't talk to me when we kiss," she declared. (The younger ones in the group laughed at this.)

"I don't *what?*" I asked, slightly dazed.

"Whenever we start kissing, we quit communicating!" she repeated more emphatically. I was beginning to see what she was getting at, but didn't want to admit it. "Well, it's kind of hard to kiss and talk at the same time."

She was right and I knew it. Whenever we limited our physical expressions, we talked to each other. We laughed, we joked, we sung, we discussed serious subjects or the totally trivial and foolish. We truly enjoyed being together and getting to know each other better. As soon as we allowed any prolonged physical contacts, we set in motion energies within us that threatened to take over our relationship. It was an extremely painful experience, but we both had to admit, at that point, we were only using each other and tempting ourselves.

"We've *got* to make out on our dates, Ken!" a misguided but honest freshman complained. "Surely you don't expect me to talk to Ted for ... let's see, he'll pick me up at seven, bring me home at midnight, that's one, two, five hours! What am I going to talk about for five hours?"

"Do you like Ted?" I asked.

Her face brightened. "Yes ... I guess I do," she answered.

"Is there any possibility that you two might get married someday?" I continued to probe.

"I'd like to think so," she replied with a broad smile.

"Hmm," I rubbed my chin with my index finger. "Isn't that interesting? You can't find enough things to talk about for five hours now. How are you going to talk with him for fifty years if you get married?"

Her smile vanished. "Oh, my," she whispered solemnly. "I never thought of that."

Talking, getting to know one another—it takes time and work, but for the couple that is looking for more than a surface relationship, it is worth the price.

Be Creative

Here's another guideline for dating: be creative in what you do and where you go. This is especially important if you are dating one person on a regular basis. Don't allow yourself to get stuck in a rut, doing the usual things all the time, going to the same old places over again.

"It's the same routine every week," complained one university coed. "A guy will call me up, invite me to a party where they're drinking, smoking, and dancing. If he can't get me drunk, he tries to get me stoned. Then I'm supposed to hop right into bed with him. That's a meaningful relationship?"

Though the plot may not be as sinister, Jan's discontent with Bill is similar. "I can almost predict our dates with clockwork regularity," she sighed. "Every week, we go to a movie, get something to eat, then go to my place. It's always the same thing. The only thing that changes is the movie!"

Creativity is an area where many couples are lazy or complacent. Granted, creative dates demand time, effort, planning, and ingenuity, but the rewards will be great to those who battle against the routine, ritual, and boredom of *spectator dates*.

Participation dates are those in which a guy and girl are activity oriented. When I was a teen, I thought the *only* acceptable "Christian dates" were those in which a lot of group action took place. My church youth group was constantly holding bowling parties, skating parties, and softball games. I was sure that they were simply trying to tire us out, so we'd be too exhausted to sin!

But there are many other kinds of opportunities. Try to reach out to others in your dating life. Take your date to an orphanage or to visit some lonely widow in an "old folks' home," or to participate in teaching, working, speaking together. There are multitudes of social-action organizations in your area that are crying out for help. Why not provide you and your date with a meaningful sharing experience, while you help someone else at the same time? This sort of time together is inexpensive, but its value to your relationship and to others is priceless.

Going Steady? Be Careful!

Though many modern young people do not view going steady as almost sacred, it cannot be denied that the consistent dating of one particular person hints that a wedding is a future possibility.

Going steady provides a person with a certain amount of social assurance. Guys don't have to face the tension and nervousness associated with asking someone out. Girls feel assured that they won't be left out or left alone. When a "big event" comes up, you don't worry whether or not you will have a date.

Going steady also usually means a certain measure of social prestige among your peer group. This is especially true of high-school dating. Once you are beyond your early twenties, our society almost expects you to be focusing on someone "special."

"When are you going to settle down and get yourself a steady girl friend, Ken?" That question used to drive me crazy.

I went steady with a girl from my freshman year of high school through my senior year. She was a lovely person; intelligent, witty, charming, well liked, and respected. I was proud to walk down the hall with her. We attended all of the local social functions and enjoyed a happy relationship.

After high school, however, we broke up. Having dated the same person for over four years, I glanced through my high school yearbook one day and thought, "Hey, I wonder what it would have been like to date Kathy? Or Joan? Or Debbie? Or Barb?" Unfortunately, Kathy, Joan, Debbie, Barb and most of the other members of my graduating class, myself included, were heading off to colleges or jobs or the service all across the country. My opportunities to develop any meaningful relationships with them were gone. Though I had enjoyed an active social life by going steady, I couldn't help feeling I had missed something.

Another reason why I do not encourage young people to go steady until they have "dated around" quite a bit is: steady dating provides too many opportunities for infatuation. True love is beautiful, but infatuation is a liar. Most young people don't know the difference.

I do not discount infatuation, or "puppy love," as it is sometimes called, when a younger couple is involved. It is a real sort of love, but it is love at its most immature level. Unfortunately many couples, teenagers and older persons as well, proceed toward marriage on the basis of puppy love, only to discover, before long, that their marriage is "a real dog."

Whatever you do, don't keep dating the same person for security's sake! True, breaking up is hard to do, but divorce is a lot worse! If you find yourself locked into a relationship that is going nowhere, get out of it, and get out of it *fast!* Be careful, though, to take every precaution that you do not devastate the other person in doing so. Basic honesty and consideration are necessary.

Heather showed me how this could be done. The "fasten your seatbelt" sign appeared aboard the jet carrying me home from a week of services in Jamaica. Heather was sitting next to me. She had been part of our mission entourage all week, but she was having trouble mustering the courage to tell me about her personal struggles, until she heard the captain signaling our trip was nearly over. She lamented, "Ken, I don't know what to do! I don't want to hurt Brian or cause him to stumble in his walk with the Lord, yet at the same time, I just don't see us together in the long run. I like him;

he's a great guy, and I don't want to lose his friendship, but I feel as though I'm stringing him along and wasting my time going steady with him."

"What are you going to do?" I asked.

"Sometimes to do the kindest thing may mean a little pain," she said, "but I'm going to tell him I think we should take some time to see others. Sure, it will hurt, but he'll get over it."

If you want to break up, don't try to "spiritualize" your actions. One girl I knew didn't have enough courage to tell her boyfriend the truth, so she blamed the ensuing breakup on God. "Well, Johnny," she told her steady, "I feel the Lord is leading me to break up with you." That's disgusting!

If you feel like you don't want to date the same person on a steady basis, let your feelings be known, gently but firmly. By the same token, if you are picking up signals indicating that your steady date may be ready for greener pastures, don't wait to get hit over the head with a two-by-four! Don't keep hanging onto a stagnant relationship; let it go. Then get back into the mainstream of the social flow. Don't go around as if in mourning for the "dearly departed."

One of the ideas I stress in my seminars is that Christian dating couples must remember that their attitudes and actions cannot be the same as those of non-Christian couples. Nowhere, or under any circumstances, are you ever free from Christ's command that you love one another just as He has loved you (John 13:34, 35; 15:12). Therefore, even in the midst of breaking off a relationship, you must demonstrate the love of Jesus. It's hard but it's possible. This is a lofty standard, to be sure, but it is imperative. Even in the midst of a breakup, the Christian is instructed to:

> Let no unwholesome word proceed from your mouth, but only such a word as is good for edification according to the need of the moment, that it may give grace to those who hear. And do not grieve the Holy Spirit of God, by whom you were sealed for the day of redemption. Let all bitterness and wrath

and anger and clamor and slander be put away from you, along with all malice. And be kind to one another, tender-hearted, forgiving each other, just as God in Christ has forgiven you.

Ephesians 4:29-32

4

Dating Non-Christians

Since one of the purposes of this book is to help you avoid being "unequally yoked together," let's plunge headlong into the controversial subject of dating between a Christian and a non-Christian. At the start, it should be pointed out that sincere men and women of God hold different views on this matter. There are those who say no Christian should ever date anyone who is not a Christian. Others see no harm in believers dating unbelievers. (I'm somewhat in the middle.)

The Ox and the Bull

Those who say a Christian should never date a non-Christian base their position squarely upon Scripture. The primary passage in this regard is found in 2 Corinthians 6:14, 15.

Do not be bound together with unbelievers; for what partnership have righteousness and lawlessness, or what fellowship has light with darkness? Or what harmony has Christ with Belial, or what has a believer in common with an unbeliever?

Certain things in life are diametrically opposed to each other, not the least of which are a believer and an unbeliever. Though the passage may yield a truth covering one's business ventures, (as well as other social ventures), it has most often been applied to dating and marriage relationships.

The words "do not be bound together," translated "do not be unequally yoked together" in the King James Version of the Bible, connote a graphic illustration. Imagine an ox and a wild bull placed within the same yoke. The ox, though strong and used to the yoke, and wanting to do the work of the master, is constantly being distracted and pulled against by the bull. The bull is not used to the yoke, and is expending huge amounts of time and energy attempting to go in a different direction, usually a direction contrary to the wishes of the master.

They are "unequally yoked together." The two are pulling against each other. There may be a lot of noise, or a lot of activity, but ultimately, the couple is getting little done for the Lord. And although they are in close proximity, neither enjoys the relationship very much! This is the picture Paul paints of the Christian who is bound together with an unbeliever.

Clearly, God is opposed to the marriage of a Christian and a non-Christian. It is a small step, then, to deduce that since it is forbidden a Christian to marry a nonbeliever, why ask for trouble by dating a non-Christian?

The answer to this problem depends upon the individual person involved, what dating means to you, and your own mental, emotional, physical, and spiritual maturity levels. What are you looking for in the dating relationship? What are your future goals, desires, and ideas on marriage? An honest evaluation of your motives may be helpful, too. If you are a born-again Christian, why do you want to date a non-Christian?

"Because there aren't any Christian guys around this town!" is usually the response I get from young women when I ask that question. In many cases, they are absolutely correct. There seem to be more Christian girls who are available for dating than there are Christian guys. If you are a single Christian man, you are sitting pretty; but single Christian women view the shortage of Christian men as a social nightmare.

"I started dating non-Christian guys out of sheer boredom," a beautiful, dark-haired, twenty-five-year-old woman told me. "I just got tired of sitting around the house waiting for a Christian man to call; those guys who were Christians and asked me out were ... well, they were sort of twinky, if you know what I mean. I decided that it would be better to date non-Christians than not to date at all."

Another Christian young woman lamented her social life. "Some people say, 'Well, just trust the Lord and have faith, and He will bring someone into your life.' That's a lot easier said than done! I trusted and waited for five years, and I had only two Christian dates during that entire period of time! Finally, I gave up the idea of dating only Christians and began to accept invitations from nonbelievers."

Can a Christian Man Be Virile?

Why does this situation exist? Many guys actually think it isn't virile to be a Christian.

One night following a Watchmen concert in Pittsburgh, I met Craig Wolfley, a walking wall of muscle. Craig is an offensive lineman for the Pittsburgh Steelers, and a devout Christian. Every week he engages in head-to-head combat with the toughest men in the National Football League. Yet Craig told me, "Following Jesus is the biggest challenge a man can ever take on!"

Slowly, but certainly, the stereotypes are being broken down. Nowadays, you can find men from all walks of life boldly proclaiming their faith in Christ. Athletes, lawyers, congressmen, businessmen, factory workers, and men from most other fields of endeavor are saying the same thing: "I have discovered the true meaning of manhood in Christ."

Though the salvation of men should thrill us all, it should cause single Christian women to nearly turn flip-flops. At last, there are some Christian guys coming on the scene! Still, the situation is changing slowly, and it may be some time before we reach anything near a balanced social equation.

Uplifting or a Downhill Slide?

What about the effects of dating nonbelievers? Some who have had this experience report that it has expanded their perspectives and even given them a greater appreciation of non-Christian attitudes and opinions, *while strengthening their own spiritual lives.*

"I knew my date would eventually get around to the subjects of religion, the Bible, and Christ," a handsome, young schoolteacher related, "so I prepared. I studied my Bible and other books, so I could answer her questions. As a result, I became much more solidly grounded in my own faith."

For others, the results of dating unbelievers have not been positive. "I really enjoyed going out with non-Christians," said a petite, blonde, young lady. "I thought it was a way to share my faith in Jesus, and often, we'd have some good discussions. Sometimes my non-Christian dates would even go to church with me. I felt that I was handling the situation pretty well.

"Then, I met Michael. Michael was not a Christian, but he was very attractive. I fell totally in love with him. Initially, he respected my values, but after dating for a couple of months, Michael's attitude changed. Gradually, he began to push for more physical activity in our relationship. I began to compromise, and slid downhill in my Christian life. When I finally gave in to Michael's desire for sex, I felt cheap and used."

Obviously, the effects of dating nonbelievers vary from person to person. It would seem that some of those who are emotionally and spiritually mature find the experience to be enriching to their own lives. For others, the practice has been devastating, and has led to a lifetime of heartache. How can we know the difference for our own lives? What are the guidelines to follow or pitfalls to be avoided?

Well, Should I or Shouldn't I?

Some people should definitely *not* date a nonbeliever. If you are a Christian who is seriously searching for a marriage partner, you'd better keep your dating within the family of God. You know God's command to "be not unequally yoked together with an unbeliever." For you to marry a non-Christian would be sinful.

Some honest soul-searching comes in handy here. Do you desire to be married? Terrific! It is a noble and admirable goal to which you have set yourself. You needn't feel ashamed or make light of your desire to be married. You have every right to want God's best for you. As a Christian, however, it is a foregone conclusion that God's best for you excludes the possibility of marrying a non-Christian.

Another person who should avoid dating non-Christians is the person who falls in love easily. If you have extremely sensitive emotions that can readily be manipulated, it would be unwise for you to place yourself in the precarious position of dating an unbeliever.

Here again, an honest appraisal of oneself is of inestimable value. Try to look at yourself realistically and objectively. Are your associations with the opposite sex based upon solid intellectual, emotional, physical, and spiritual responses to the other person; or are you the type of person whose heart begins to palpitate madly every time a potential date looks your way?

If "Mr. [or Miss] Wonderful" is not a Christian, you may find yourself suddenly forced to choose between the love of Christ and your love for that person. It's a poor and painful choice.

With all this in mind, let's ask the question, "What are you going to do if you fall in love with a non-Christian?" What would *you* do?

When I have posed this question at seminars, one typical answer is, "Well, I'll just make sure I don't fall in love with him [or her]." That is a terribly naive solution to a serious problem. Love and sexual attraction are two of the most powerful forces in the world.

The fact is: Christians do fall in love with nonbelievers. Many deeply committed Christians have played Russian Roulette with their emotions—and have lost. They fell in love with nonbelievers, willfully chose to disobey God's Word, and went ahead with marriages that God has opposed. You cannot compromise God's Word and still expect His blessing!

I frequently hear, "But I know a Christian who married a non-Christian, and they are extremely happy together." No doubt, this is sometimes true, but, can any Christian really be happy knowing that he has willfully disobeyed the command of God? And, what happens to the relationship between the believing partner and his Lord? Many times it is seriously disrupted. A third question is, "What do you mean by 'happiness'?" For a Christian, there is no such thing as joy, peace, *or* happiness outside of God's will for his life. Would you really want to be bound to someone who could not comprehend the Gospel's life-encompassing implications, could not share with you the intimate feelings of your faith? And what about the unbeliever? If the couple breaks up, what impression will he or she have of the Christian's God? "What kind of God would want to destroy something so beautiful?" The standards of Christianity always appear as foolishness to those who are perishing (1 Corinthians 1:18).

Perhaps the most common idea Christians have when they begin to date or if they marry a non-Christian is: *I'll convert him!* But there is no guarantee. It seems the devil has deceived many into believing that it will somehow be easier to persuade an unbeliever to become a Christian *after* you are married. But thousands of Christians who have lived with or are living with a non-Christian mate will bear witness to the fact that it is not easier to convert an unbelieving mate after the wedding.

Let me tell you one little story. One night an older woman was rejoicing at the close of an evangelistic service at which I was speaking. Her joy was so obvious, I felt compelled to ask the reason for her elation.

"My husband, my husband!" she exclaimed through tears of joy. "He became a Christian tonight!"

"Terrific!" I responded. "How long have you been married?"

"Thirty-eight years," she replied. "And tonight, for the first time, we're a family!" Great tears of joy flowed freely from that dear woman's eyes, as her husband and three children joined her in an embrace.

My own heart was thrilled at the sight of a family that had been brought together spiritually for the first time. Nevertheless, I felt a twinge of sadness to their story. *Thirty-eight years!* I thought. *That's a long time to be living together as man and wife and never know the spiritual intimacy of coming together with Christ in the center of the home.*

The plain fact is a simple one. Spiritual incompatibility heightens the possibility of divorce. Statistics prove it. God does not want you to suffer the pain of a broken marriage. He does not delight in watching you live a life of divided loyalties. That is why He has given us definite guidelines to help us before the enemy attacks these unguarded areas of our lives. You have no guarantee that a non-Christian mate will ever become a Christian, so why take chances? Be careful who you date; be careful with your heart. God places a much higher premium upon our *obedience* than He does our superficial happiness.

Why is spiritual incompatibility important? Remember that the two of you live in different worlds. Without Christ directing you both, your attitudes toward dating, love, sex, marriage, and the purpose of life itself are at odds.

This is a tenet of Christianity that many people find difficult to accept. We would rather allow the distinctions between a Christian and non-Christian to become blurred, minimized, or even totally ignored. After all, it is difficult to be popular on the social scene if one is branded as "different." Yet Jesus poignantly demands that we be a counterculture within a culture. He tells us straightforwardly, "If you were of the world, the world would love its own; but because you are not of the world, but I chose you out of the world, therefore the world hates you" (John 15:19).

Dating on Thin Ice

Nowhere is this truth more vulnerable to compromise than in our social relationships. Yet it is precisely here we Christians need to hold the distinctions even more dearly. To neglect to do so is to open ourselves to trouble, disillusionment, and heartache.

If you are a Christian who chooses to date an unbeliever, you must keep in mind that you begin each date from a completely dissimilar mind-set. Your entire value systems are likely to be different. To you, marriage is an honorable estate, ordained and blessed by God. To the non-Christian, the wedding may be nothing more than a ceremony and a piece of paper that make it socially acceptable for two people to live together. To you, sex may be the ultimate expression between two people who love each other and are pledged to each other for life. To the unbeliever, sex may be nothing more than the carrying out of the natural instincts, doing that which feels good. To the Christian, love is an unconditional act of the will that is both the initiator and result of a total commitment between two people. To the non-Christian, love may be a temporary, transitory expression, loosely binding two people together. A popular phrase in many current secular wedding ceremonies belies this lack of firm commitment when it asserts, "as long as the two shall love." These differences pervade the entire relationship.

Let's be honest. It's tough enough nowadays for two Christians to maintain a pure and holy relationship, let alone a Christian and a non-Christian. Even with two deeply devoted children of God who are working together to do what is pleasing in His sight, there remain monumental pressures and temptations to be conquered.

Another risk you run in dating a non-Christian is the risk of falling out of fellowship with other Christians, and eventually even losing your relationship with Christ. Do not be deceived by your own spiritual overconfidence or idealism.

Solomon was one of the wisest and wealthiest men who ever lived. He was the successor to King David's throne in Israel. He had everything he could possibly want, including his pick of the most beautiful women in the nation. Moreover, God had chosen Solomon to play a unique role in the salvation of the world. His was a blessed life, to say the least!

Yet, Solomon had one great shortcoming: he had a penchant for ungodly women. Though he was greatly blessed by God, and he had an intimate friendship with the Lord, Solomon lost it all because he got involved with nonbelieving women.

> For it came about when Solomon was old, his wives turned his heart away after other gods; and his heart was not wholly devoted to the Lord. . . .
>
> 1 Kings 11:4

Because of this man's disobedience, God tore the nation of Israel into pieces, and took the throne away from Solomon's immediate family. Not only did Solomon lose out with God because of his entanglement with ungodly women, so also did his children and the entire nation!

Have you heard comments that go like this:

> "Yeah, sure. I'll go to church with you tonight. But then afterwards, why don't we stop down at the lounge for a few drinks? I hear they have a great new band there."

"Do you mean we are going to double with those fuddy-duddies again? Why don't we go out with Grace and Bob? They really know what's happening!"

"All you ever want to do is go to church! When are we going to the lake? Sunday morning; Sunday nights; Wednesday-night prayer meetings; Thursday's choir practice; Saturday visitations! Are you in love with me or that church?"

Dating non-Christians will almost always create a drag on your spiritual life. Soon, it becomes easier to neglect the activities of your church and the fellowship of other believers. Other involvements crowd out your devotional life. Your Bible lies unopened, and the time you formerly spent in prayer is consumed by something else. Even the time that you do spend in church or Bible study or in prayer proves unproductive.

The Price Is *Wrong!*

In light of these risks, intrinsic to the experience of dating a non-believer, any genuine Christian must ask the question, "Is it really worth it?" Is *anything* worth it if it jeopardizes one's relationship with Jesus Christ?

I began the discussion of Christians dating non-Christians by stating that I feel it is possible for some people to engage in "mixed dating" and to walk away with lives unscathed, and, perhaps, even enriched. I must confess, however, that I advise most of the young people I counsel to avoid the practice.

I firmly believe that dating between two *Christians* is far more fun anyhow! There are whole vistas that can be shared between two believers, even on a casual date. The chances of enjoying a meaningful dating experience, one that is pleasurable for both members of the couple and one that is pleasing in the sight of our heavenly Father, are greatly enhanced when two Christians are working together toward the same goal.

Part II

What's Love Got To Do With It? (Love, Sex, and Temptation)

5

Looking for Love

One of the most popular songs of 1984 was Tina Turner's "What's Love Got to Do With It?" ... sex, that is. "Everything," a Christian would answer. "Nothing," she seems to imply. And that's what the world often thinks today. Tune in any pop radio station and you can hear songs of love dozens of times every hour. Love poetry, good and bad, abounds. Turn on your television set, go to a movie, pick up a magazine, and inevitably, you will be confronted by "love."

What Is This Thing Called Love?

But what *is* love? Try to define it. Even the best descriptions and definitions seem to be grasping at air.

Of course, there are different types and degrees of love. There is love for God, love for country, and love of family. Some people "love" everything from baseball to Big Macs.

I want to discuss the kind of love that relates to the building of a permanent relationship between one man and one woman. Dr. Charlie Shedd calls this "marriageable love" in *How to Know If You're Really in Love.*

Speaking of this kind of love, the Bible holds forth one of the most beautiful descriptions of love that has ever been proclaimed. The Apostle Paul's words to the first-century church at Corinth can hardly be improved upon.

Love is patient, love is kind, and is not jealous; love does not brag and is not arrogant, does not act unbecomingly; it does not seek its own, is not provoked, does not take into account a wrong suffered, does not rejoice in unrighteousness, but rejoices with the truth; bears all things, believes all things, hopes all things, endures all things.

Love never fails. . . .

1 Corinthians 13:4–8

Now that's the kind of love a married couple needs!

Love Comes in Three Degrees

The ancient Greek language (in which Paul wrote) had three words for love. One of these, *eros*, connotes sexual or passionate love. From this root word we get our word *erotic*. This word is used in the twentieth century to describe much of the permissive sensuality and warped sexual practices that are being passed off as love. The apostle Paul, however, never once used this word in 1 Corinthians, chapter 13. In fact, you will not find this word for *love* used in the New Testament at all!

The second Greek word that can be translated as love is *phileo*. This sort of love is often characterized as brotherly love or deep friendship. The name of the city Philadelphia, called the "city of brotherly love," derives from this word.

Paul, however, chose a different word to speak of love. The word the apostle used is *agape*. This is the highest and most noble sort of love. It is a *self-giving* rather than *self-seeking* love. This is God's kind of love. It is the kind of love that He has for each of us. And it is the kind of love He wants us to have for each other.

This sort of love has at least two vital elements at its foundation: *unconditional acceptance of the other person,* and a *creative quality* that causes two people to stimulate each other to greater growth. *Agape love* does not seek to change the other person. If you really love someone, you are willing to accept the person just the way he or she is. Yet an amazing characteristic of this unconditional love is the creativity and constructive capacity for change it usually brings.

This does not mean that it is wrong for you to envision noble dreams for your partner. On the contrary, in a truly worthwhile relationship, there should be a deep desire to see your date or mate "put his [or her] best foot forward," and be everything he or she can possibly be.

Nor does acceptance mean that a person in love should be blind to the faults, errors, weaknesses, and sins of the other person. The exact opposite is true. Love sees; love knows; love is painfully aware of the failures and faults of the other person. Yet, miracle of miracles, love loves on, in spite of these things. If you cannot love your partner, "warts and all," it is highly unlikely that your relationship is grounded in true love. Certainly, you may fall far short of this standard at times. It takes years of sacrificial work to develop such a relationship. But press on toward that glorious goal!

How Do You Know You're in Love?

The Watchmen were working on an album with producer Brown Bannister in Nashville. As we listened to the playback of one of our most popular songs, "True Love Never Fails," Brown suddenly punched the STOP button. The flashing lights and bouncing needles of the multitrack studio equipment fell dark and motionless.

Brown looked at me across the console and asked, "How can you know for sure whether or not love is real?"

I was touched by the sincerity of his question. And unfortunately, I had no pat answers. There are no simple *A, B, C* formulas that you can use to gauge your love. You cannot put human relationships to a litmus test. There are only two things that provide any sort of guarantee at all: *time* and *prayer.* If you will give your relationship the necessary time to develop, the truth about your love will become obvious. If you will nurture your growing love with prayer, you can have perfect confidence that God is deeply concerned about your relationship and has promised to guide and direct you to the correct decision.

However, some relatively simple soul-searching can help you decide whether or not your love is of marriageable quality.

What a Body! An honest answer to a frank question could possibly keep the two of you from making a serious error concerning your future. The question is, "Do I really love my partner, or do I merely enjoy his [or her] body?" While it is true that the physical aspects of a relationship are important, physical appeal should never be the primary reason for love or marriage.

Sammy Tippit, a popular youth speaker, rightly points out, in *You, Me, He,* "If you are in love with someone's body (and someday you should be) but not his mind and spirit, you are not truly in love. If the best thing you can say about your 'loved' one is that he or she is 'foxy,' you're in trouble. True love engulfs the total person."

Gimme Some Respect! I seriously question whether love can exist where there is no respect, one person for the other. Mutual respect is one of the foundational building blocks upon which true love will stand or fall.

Respect implies an appreciation and admiration for your partner. Even if no one else in the world can see a reason to appreciate your partner, *you* can! In your partner's moment of greatest triumph or worst defeat, when he or she causes pride to well up within you (or embarrassment to envelop you), true love continues to respect its partner.

If you find yourself prone to tearing your partner down in order to build yourself up, you can be certain you do not have a good future together. True love will always seek to edify and uplift the other person.

Be careful of your jokes, and especially of cutting sarcasm, in this regard. Be honest; listen to your humor. Who is the real recipient of its striking edge? If you find it to be your potential marriage partner, you'd better straighten out your humor or find yourself a new mate. True love never enjoys seeing its partner made out to be a fool.

Are You a Giver or a Getter? If you are in the midst of a relationship where you are constantly trying to "get" something from your partner, it is obvious that your feelings are being controlled by lust, not love. Lust always seeks its own fulfillment, its own gratification. Love looks to preserve the interests of the other person. Love is never selfish.

This sort of unselfish love does not happen overnight. Many times it takes years to develop. Still, if you do not at least feel yourself moving in this direction and see signs that your partner is moving in a similar pattern, you would be wise to discontinue your relationship. Two people using each other for their own fulfillment is not God's idea of true love.

Dr. Dennis Kinlaw, while president of Asbury College, aptly cautioned young people to beware of the person who says, "I want you; I need you." This, said Dr. Kinlaw, is not real love.

A quick review of the pronouns such a person uses will reveal his or her true motives to be selfish and egocentric.

I Won't Last a Day Without You. If your love cannot exist apart from physical expressions, you'd better watch out! You may not be in love with your partner; you might be "in lust."

My brothers' and my involvement in the Watchmen keeps us "on the road" for days, sometimes even weeks at a time. My eldest brother, John, has been married to Sandy for many years. All days totaled, however, he has probably spent less than half of those years at home! In their case, a love that is solely contingent upon constant physical proximity and intimate expressions would soon die.

What Are You Building? True love seeks to build a relationship. Love, at its best, can never be an overnight affair. Real love seeks to know another person deeply and intimately. To know and to be known are admirable goals for all true lovers. This type of love involves two essential elements: *honest transparency* and *real communication.*

By *transparency,* I mean the ability of two people to come together, faults and all, in open acceptance of each other. Of course, this sort of relationship presents some real risks. "Suppose I open myself to her, and she doesn't like what she sees?" "If I allow him to see what I'm really like, he may not want me!" To these fears I can only answer that it is far better to discover each other's true self early in the relationship than later. Furthermore, if a couple will seek to develop an agape type of love, the foibles and failures of the individual partners can be met, accepted, and conquered.

This is not an instant-success formula. Knowing and allowing yourself to be known is a continual process. It is something you must work at. The best dating or marriage relationship is that in which a couple is constantly in a state of rediscovering each other.

Communication is the key. I do not simply mean talking *at* another person. If your relationship is to have any future, there must be sincere sharing with your partner. You must be able to interact with each other in absolute truthfulness. If you find yourself prone to exaggeration, lies, or half-truths, or suspect your partner of such, it is obvious that the two of you have a definite communication problem (not to mention a spiritual problem! *See* Ephesians 4:25).

Practically speaking, communication implies that each partner has something to share. If you are trying to discern whether or not your love is of marriageable quality, an incisive question should be considered: Can you carry on a serious and lengthy conversation together? Many couples can only talk together for a few minutes on a superficial level, after which they find their well of conversation running dry.

Lasting communication requires a large measure of common interests. Often, partners have problems because their interests are so dissimilar. Each gets wrapped up in his or her own activity, much to the dismay of the other partner.

You probably know people who are merely going through the motions of playing husband and wife. He is constantly preoccupied with his work, and she is preoccupied with her friends and her child. They are married and living in the same house, but that is the extent of their relationship.

True love requires *genuine* communication. A couple must share the most important parts of their lives with each other. A love that can find nothing to say will soon die.

Can You Accept Responsibilities? True love also accepts responsibilities. There are many people nowadays who say that we are accountable only to our own selves. They carry this sort of thinking into all their social relationships. "Do your own thing" is the prevailing philosophy of modern culture. "If it feels good, do it!" shouts at our society's collective psyche from television, radio, "literature," movies, and billboards. "Don't worry about anyone else; take care of Number One first."

This attitude is diametrically opposed to the teachings of Christ and self-defeating in our social relationships. Real love demands responsibility, and responsibility implies a genuine concern for what is ultimately the best for each member of a couple. If this is not the prevailing attitude in your relationship, beware! You may be dooming yourself to a future of unhappiness and heartache.

Walter Trobisch wisely pointed out in *I Loved a Girl* that the responsibility involved in true love is not simply one person for the other, but rather, both are responsible before God.

> Where love is, you no longer say "I," but "you"; I am responsible for you. You are responsible for me. Together then you stand before God where you do not say "you and I," but rather "we."

The pattern of assuming responsibility must begin in the dating process. Don't expect a marriage vow to produce a transformation in this area, if you and your partner are unwilling to accept responsibilities before your wedding day.

Start in the small, seemingly insignificant areas, to develop a practice of taking responsibility. For example, if there is a certain time that you know you should be in from a date, either because of your job, or parental requirements, or your own physical limitations, make a sincere effort to get home within your deadline.

If you have set limits upon your physical expressions for each other (and every dating couple should), do not violate your principles or those of your partner. Take an active role in maintaining standards; don't assume that your partner will take this responsibility.

Either E-go or I-go! True love does not depend upon *ego gratification.* In this regard, I am referring to the myriad ways in which we all strive to be recognized, acknowledged, and appreciated. These are natural desires and are quite appropriate so long as they are not given a higher priority than they deserve. Although, when a person is truly in love, his or her love does not demand to be noticed or praised for every little unselfish act toward the other person.

This is a totally foreign concept in a society gone mad with self-centeredness. We are schooled in methods to attract attention to ourselves, either by the way we look, the way we talk, or the way we act. It is extremely rare to find a person who is willing to give of himself without the expectation of reward or recognition.

Yet this is precisely the type of love exhibited by the life of Jesus Christ and described by the apostle Paul in First Corinthians, chapter 13. True love loves whether or not it is noticed, appreciated, or returned.

Does this sound like a difficult dimension of love? Let me assure you that it is. A twenty-seven-year-old man I met recently at one of my seminars shed some light on this truth for me.

"When Susan first told me that she loved me, I cringed a little. I didn't know if I was ready for that. I had been hurt before, and I wasn't about to risk being hurt by love again. Gradually, I began to let go of the reins that had restricted my feelings. I began to express my love to her in various ways.

"Suddenly, Susan began to pull back. She still claimed to love me, but she was less expressive about it, and didn't return the love that I was extending. It was the most horrible feeling I had ever known! It was like climbing onto the edge of a tree limb, then looking back to see someone cutting off the limb!

"At first, I could feel only the pains of hurt and rejection all over again. I both loved and hated that girl. I felt that she was flippantly fooling with my feelings.

"It was then that the Lord began to teach me that true love does not demand a return. In fact, I concluded that if my love was based solely on her response to me, my feelings were conditional and self-seeking, and perhaps, not love at all!"

Indeed, this dimension of love is often difficult. On the other hand, when love is genuine, this aspect of love is precious to experience and delightful to see in action.

Two friends of mine have such an effective marriage they have become a model for me. They have been married seven years. It is beautiful to see how they express their love for each other. Not simply in words, caresses, or kisses; they show their feelings toward one another with little selfless acts. They are constantly doing things for each other, as the natural result of the deep love they share. They do not seem to be even conscious of doing these things. There is no effort to conjure up these expressions of love. They are not conditional acts. They are not done to persuade or obligate the other person. Their care for one another is simply the inevitable result of God's agape kind of love being unleashed in their lives.

All or Nothing! Ultimately, true love requires total commitment. This is more than gushy, mushy feelings. True love stems not from the emotions, but rather from the will. A person truly in love must be willing to say to his or her partner, "You are the one I want. You're the one I want to live for. I've made up my mind. From now on, for as long as I live, I give myself totally to you, to the exclusion of all others." True love demands this complete and irrevocable decision to willfully give oneself to another. To make such a radical pledge of oneself to another person seems unrealistic and untenable to most who have grown up in the "light" of our permissive and noncommittal society.

Of course, on your own strength, in your own power (even with sincere intentions), this sort of commitment seems impossible. After all, who knows what the future may hold? You may not be the same person ten years from now that you are today. How can you commit yourself for tomorrows, when you can barely cope with today?

It is precisely at this point that we are able to see the glaring differences between God's agape kind of love and man's selfish love. Man's love says, "I love you *if* you meet a certain set of conditions and *if* you continue to meet those conditions in the future. I love you *because* of a certain set of circumstances and *if* those circumstances remain the same in the future, I will continue to love you."

The obvious question should spring into every thinking person's mind. "What if those conditions or circumstances change in the future? What happens to our love then?" Surely, if love is going to last, it must be grounded upon something more than feelings, appearances, or other temporary conditions.

It is here that Christianity provides a better alternative. Jesus Christ has offered to put within us a supernatural love—His love, God's agape love. He gave us the ultimate demonstration of this sort of love by committing Himself to die upon a cross in our stead. The Bible states explicitly, "But God demonstrates His own love toward us, in that while we were yet sinners, Christ died for us" (Romans 5:8). Furthermore, since God demonstrated such a love for us, we, in turn, should demonstrate a similar sort of love for each other (1 John 4:11).

A good check to determine the depth and degree of our love might be: "Am I willing to give up my life for my partner?" To me, that sort of love is not astounding. In fact, that is God's idea of a "normal" love.

In a truly successful, loving relationship, one of the main ingre dients is the willingness of the partners to place the needs, desires, and welfare of each other ahead of themselves. Where this principle is mutually practiced by a couple, there is love, harmony, and respect. When this principle is ignored, incessant friction, fighting, bitterness, and often, even deep-seated hatred breeds unabated.

Not only is Jesus Christ our example of selfless, total commitment in love, He is also our enabler for this sort of love. It is impossible to make a total commitment to another person apart from His love in us. All human efforts, regardless how noble, will fall far short of this supernaturally endowed love.

Here, then, is an extremely strange but wonderful paradox! In the perfect love affair, there are not *two* people involved, but *three!* You and your partner are involved, of course, but for the richest and most lasting sort of love possible this side of heaven, the relationship must include a third party. It is, in fact, that third party who is able to keep the two of you immeasurably in love with each other for a lifetime and beyond. The third party in the perfect love affair is, of course, Jesus Christ.

Well, how did you fare? Are you really in love? In light of the above standards, is your partner really in love with *you?*

Should you find that you and your partner have a relationship that falls far short of the above standards, you have but two choices. Either commit yourselves to a radical redevelopment program, or else forget the relationship entirely. If the two of you are not willing to work toward bettering your relationship, you are not in love. You may be attracted to each other. Perhaps you may be involved in a relationship of convenience or something else. One thing is certain: *you are not in love.* Here's the point at which Paul Simon's song should be employed. There are "fifty ways to leave your lover." False love is the kind you want to leave behind.

6

Our *R*-Rated Society

A few years ago, to begin my seminars on the subject of "Sex and the Single Person," I painstakingly sought to prove to my audiences that we were living in the midst of a major upheaval of our sexual values.

That is no longer necessary.

The "Sexual Revolution," as it has been called, has so successfully pulled off its coup, it is no longer even considered revolutionary. The so-called New Morality has been with us for so long, it now seems old hat.

An entire generation has grown up in or grown accustomed to our *R*-rated society. Premarital sex, extramarital sex, group sex, kinky sex, any and every kind of sex is readily available in nearly every city in America. Pornography abounds. Television programs and movies are increasingly explicit in their presentations of the erotic. Homosexuality is advocated as a "normal alternative way of life." Incidents of rape, illegitimate babies, and abortions are all occurring with mounting frequency, but the soaring statistics hardly raise an eyebrow nowadays.

"You've Got to Be Kidding!"

Consequently, even devout Christian young people are questioning the old codes of morality and biblical standards. This phenomenon is not unique to our generation. God's people have often questioned, doubted, and even ignored His Word in the past. They have always done so at their own peril and expense. However, the idea that we can choose to ignore God's clear teaching concerning our sexuality, that we can willfully disobey His commands without marring or fracturing our relationship with Him, is an extremely dangerous effect the New Morality's ethical teachings have had upon our attitudes and conduct.

So far has society drifted from its biblical moorings that many modern Christian young people are shocked at the exclusiveness of God's commands concerning our sex lives.

"Do you mean to tell me that it's really important to God for me to have sex with only one person in my life?" a sarcastic collegian asked me.

"Yep," I answered. "That's exactly what I mean."

"You've got to be kidding!" he replied, shaking his head as he walked away, carrying a Bible under his arm.

Granted, God's book on sexuality is quite different from *Playboy* or *Cosmopolitan.* The difference is both complex and simple. While the latter two magazines extol immediate gratification, God's Word concerning our sexuality was given so we might discover the maximum fulfillment and enjoyment that sex can bring to our lives.

Forbidden Fruit

I was speaking on this subject at a conference in New York when I made the statement, "There is nothing wrong with sex."

A young woman sitting in the front row enthusiastically agreed with me. "Hey, hey, hey! All *right!*" she crowed.

"God is not against sex," I continued, matter-of-factly.

"Yeah! Right! Preach it, Ken!" she hooted. She sat on the edge of her seat, and everyone was waiting to hear what I would say next.

"But," I began, "God is definitely against the misuse of sex!" I finished emphatically.

"Oh," she barely whispered, as she sagged in her seat, looking like a deflated balloon.

God always speaks favorably and lovingly about the sexual relationship *when* it is performed within the context for which He designed it. That context, of course, is marriage. Wait a minute! Before you throw up your hands in frustration, let me remind you that God wants you to have a *super* sex life!

Yet the Bible condemns *all* sexual conduct outside the bonds of the marriage relationship. It labels all such conduct as sin. It labels those who engage in such conduct as adulterers and fornicators, and says that God pours out His wrath upon them.

Wrath? Isn't the guilt, potential pregnancy, abortion, disease and such, a good description of wrath? Certainly! But it gets worse!

> ... Do not be deceived; neither fornicators, nor idolaters, nor adulterers, nor effeminate, nor homosexuals ... shall inherit the Kingdom of God.
>
> 1 Corinthians 6:9,10

I am not trying to frighten you into being "good." The Puritans tried that approach and failed. Fear will only guide a person's moral choices for so long. Sexual desire will overcome fear, anyhow, unless guided by a higher principle.

The Master's Plan

Don't let anyone deceive you! God is not vague concerning your sexual conduct. His Word is not ambiguous when it comes to help-

ing us develop a definite system of sexual ethics. A review of a few
Scriptures will reinforce God's standards in our minds.

> Do not let immorality or any impurity or greed even be
> named among you, as is proper among saints. . . . For this you
> know with certainty, that no immoral or impure person or
> covetous man, who is an idolater, has an inheritance in the
> kingdom of Christ and God.
>
> Ephesians 5:3,5

> Therefore consider the members of your earthly body as dead
> to immorality, impurity, passion, evil desire and greed, which
> amounts to idolatry.
>
> Colossians 3:5

Note, in both passages, God equates sexual sin with idolatry. As
such, when one commits immorality, he not only breaks God's
Commandment, "You shall not commit adultery"; he also breaks
the First Commandment, "You shall have no other gods before
Me," and the Second Commandment, as well, "You shall not make
for yourself an idol . . . (Exodus 20:3,4). The implication is that in
sexual sin, the person is worshiping the created order rather than
the Creator.

My favorite passage concerning our sexual conduct is found in 1
Thessalonians, chapter four. J. B. Phillips catches the tenor of the
passage when he translates:

> God's plan is to make you holy, and that means a clean cut
> with sexual immorality. Every one of you should learn to
> control his body, keeping it pure and treating it with re-
> spect. . . .
>
> 1 Thessalonians 4:3,4 PHILLIPS

This passage links our sexual attitudes and conduct with the holy
life to which God has called us. You can tell a great deal about a

person's spiritual life by the way he or she handles the sacred area of sexuality.

But, to go back to the question that college guy asked me at the beginning of this chapter, why should God care? Why does God give us such strict regulations concerning our sexuality? Is He an old fuddy-duddy who doesn't want us to enjoy one of life's greatest pleasures? Is He trying to cramp our style? Does He want to hurt us, to make us miserable, to keep us frustrated all the time? No, the truth is that God wants us to enjoy every gift He gives us. In order to do this, He has given us rules and regulations for their use and our own good, so we won't hurt ourselves, and don't harm others.

God's Word is extremely logical. His plan for your life works when you follow His instructions. His plan for sexual relations is a workable one, not simply an ideal at which to aim. When you live your life according to His will, you are happy. When you choose to disobey, you are miserable.

7

Almost Paradise

The most important reason for abstaining from sexual immorality is simply stated: *God said so!* But there are many practical, nitty-gritty reasons for handling our bodies according to His Word. Let's look at the rationale behind the rules.

Previews of Coming Attractions

The initial attraction between a man and a woman usually has sexual overtones. I'm sure there are those who would say, "No, my initial attraction to Mabel was due to her intellect." You might say, "It was the way he treated his dog that first attracted me to Herman." More often, though, I have heard comments like, "Wow, what a gorgeous body he has!" or, "I just love the way she moves!"

"Her eyes just seem to melt me."

"His touch sent shivers all up and down my back."

Sound familiar?

This initial sexual attraction, based almost entirely upon our physical senses, is not wrong. In fact, God designed things to be just that way. We are sexual beings. Our Creator intended that we should be physically attracted to our opposite sex.

There are, however, tensions and frustrations within every couple that are directly related to sexual attraction. This is true whether you are two fourteen-year-olds on a first date, or two adults who have been dating for months or even years. How you deal with these sexual pressures will, to a great extent, determine your future sexual happiness and, possibly, the future of the relationship itself.

Frustrating, but Rewarding. Picture this. Nobody else is home. You and the one you love are wrapped in each other's arms on the living-room sofa. You are theoretically watching television—but it's been at least an hour since you heard even the noisiest, most blaring commercial.

You want to touch. You want to explore each other's body. You want to feel the warmth of your flesh pressed together.

Something tells you that you are heading for trouble if you continue. Maybe the Holy Spirit causes something to flash across your mind that you read or heard concerning the logical reasons for sexual restraint. In any case, you say to yourself, *Hey, we've got to cool it!*

Right at this point, your sexual frustration level is running at near-fever pitch. You have a choice to make. You can let your sexual desires run their natural course, or you can put the brakes on, redirect the activity of the moment, and come away from the situation with the satisfaction of knowing that you just resisted one of the most difficult temptations known to the human race.

Most of our society, when confronted with this choice, would say, "What? Are you crazy? Go for it! Do it!"

On the other hand, the Christian single person says, "No, I'm going to sacrifice the pleasure of the moment for a better and more lasting pleasure in the future." (Or words to that effect!)

If you go ahead and engage in sexual activity outside of the marriage commitment, you will admittedly dissolve some of the frustration of waiting. At the same time, however, you will also destroy part of the God-ordained sexual tension that was attracting you and your partner in the first place!

After the Lovin'. One guy revealed to me, "I knew our relationship was built on nothing but blatant lust, when after we made love, I couldn't stand to see her. I didn't want her near me; she wanted me to hold her and caress her, but I was totally turned off by shame and guilt."

It's a sad story, isn't it? What makes it worse is the fact that it is repeated over and over again in the lives of modern young people.

Trust and *respect* are the keys. The tensions and frustrations of "waiting until marriage" can be a definite plus for a couple. At a Nashville concert, while waiting backstage for the Watchmen's cue, a well-known musician divulged certain secrets of his dating past to me.

"Long before my wife and I were married, we were both born-again Christians. When we started dating, we had definite ideas about sex and how we wanted to handle it. We agreed to keep our dating life acceptable in God's sight. We both were acquainted with His standards so it was no big problem at first.

"However, as we continued to date over a long period of time, the physical pressures got tougher to deal with. We enjoyed kissing and touching, just like any other couple, but we knew that we were playing with fire. We began to take steps to 'cool it' in regard to the physical aspects of our relationship.

"Nowadays it seems unpopular to say so, but I always feel proud when I tell someone that my wife and I did not have sex before we were married. A lot of my musician friends still think I'm either lying or crazy. They can't imagine a beautiful relationship without having sex before marriage.

"Call it old-fashioned if you want to, but I know that because I respected her and we didn't have sex before we were married, we trust each other a lot more now that we are married. On the road, there are all sorts of sexual temptations, even for a Christian. Some people have asked me, 'Doesn't your wife worry about all those pretty girls around at your concerts?' I tell them, 'Nope. She knew she could trust me before we were married, and she can still trust me now. I feel the same way about her.'"

If you or your partner or both are unwilling to sacrifice now so the two of you can have a better relationship in the future, it is a clear sign of immaturity and selfishness. It's a good clue that one who cannot control his sexual desires, quite likely cannot control his or her temper, tongue, pride, greed, financial dealings, or many other facets of his or her life. To selfishly seek to satisfy your desires every time your sexual motor gets turned on is not proof of power or a sign of strength, virility, or assertiveness. It is actually an indication of weakness.

Walter Trobisch likens this situation to an automobile. Trobisch points out that it is simple to manipulate the gas pedal. Anyone can do that. A child can. Some animals could. To learn how to handle the steering wheel and the brakes is another problem completely (*I Loved a Girl*).

So it is with our sexuality. To control sex takes all the willpower you've got. It may be tough at times. You will need to draw upon every moral fiber within you and still find it necessary to call out to God for His supernatural help. But the frustrations and tensions you encounter and overcome in the process will help mold you into a much better person as a result.

Uncommittedly Yours

One of the lies concerning premarital sex is that by exploring each other's sexuality, a couple is better equipped for marriage.

"How will we know whether we are sexually compatible if we don't try things out first?" a chemistry major asked me on one campus where the Watchmen were in concert. To him, it made sense to "experiment" before drawing any conclusions.

But what does *compatible* mean here? It is a medical fact that nearly every couple *can* be sexually compatible if they will take the time to educate themselves and adjust to each other. Tim Stafford agrees:

> The problems most couples have with sex relate strongly to other parts of their relationship—their ability to communi-

cate, their willingness to be unselfish in love, and their understanding and love for their partner ... To stay exciting, sex
requires an exciting, growing relationship. Nothing you do in
bed before marriage tests that!

A Love Story

"Hold it, Ken!" a lot of young people object at this point. "You
say that good sex before marriage doesn't necessarily result in good
sex within marriage. Wouldn't it be smart to live together for a
while on a trial basis to see if things are going to work?"

Not really. To enjoy fulfilled sex, two factors are indispensable to
the relationship. One is *time* and the other is *commitment.*

The time factor is important because it often takes so much of it
before a couple can really settle into a satisfying sex life together.
For some couples, this takes weeks; for others, it takes months; for
some it takes years. In order for a couple to adapt to each other,
each partner needs to know that he or she will be given all the time
necessary to develop a sex life that is pleasurable for both.

Josh McDowell says, "A good sex life very seldom produces a
good relationship. But I know one thing: a good marriage produces
a fantastic sex life, because sex is the result of a good relationship
rather than the cause of it" (*Giver, Takers*).

Of course, McDowell is talking about sex within the confines of a
total, irrevocable commitment between two people who love each
other. When a couple is living together without the marriage vows,
this commitment simply does not exist. What kind of a commitment
is it when one or both of the partners can walk away at any time, no
strings attached?

The wise Christian knows that sex can be "enjoyed in its fullest
only under the auspices of publicly acknowledged permanent commitment—i.e., a marriage. Intercourse should be more than
scratching a genital itch, appeasing hormonal passions. It is, the
Bible says, 'the language of oneness,' " as Stephen Board declares in
Guide to Sex, Singleness & Marriage.

Josh McDowell concludes, "This unity in sexual intercourse provides for a man and woman the most lasting enjoyment and maximum fulfillment they can possibly know" (*Givers, Takers*).

Outside the marriage commitment, even the most noble intentions are just that: intentions. Tim was a student at a Bible college, studying for the ministry. Judy was a talented musician with a beautiful voice. They were engaged to be married right after their graduation from college.

During their senior year of school, Tim and Judy were invited to minister at many off-school churches. Unfortunately, they did not practice what they proclaimed. On the way back to campus, they would often stop at a motel to indulge in sexual intimacies. At first, they restricted themselves to heavy petting, but as their relationship went on, they eventually progressed to intercourse. They justified their behavior on the basis that they would soon be married.

"What difference do a piece of paper and a ceremony make?" they rationalized. "As far as we are concerned, we're married now. We just haven't had a public wedding yet."

Their story is predictable. You guessed it. They broke up. The engagement ring was returned to the jeweler, and life was supposed to go on as usual.

The only problem was that neither of them could quite continue life as normal, even after confessing their sins and asking for forgiveness from God and each other.

"Every time I would see Tim on campus," Judy confessed, "I would feel cheap." Judy finally couldn't take it anymore. She dropped out of college with less than a semester to go before graduation. The last time I saw her she was working in a menial job, her talent for singing wasted.

Tim suffered similar consequences. "Even after I knew I was forgiven by God and by Judy, the pain was still there," he told me. "We thought sex was okay because we were engaged. Man, were we wrong! After we broke up, it was awful. Every time I saw Judy, my insides felt like they were going to come undone. We were both virgins before she and I started dating. If we had waited, we'd probably be together today!"

Engagement Is Not Marriage. The case of Tim and Judy points out a sobering truth, namely: engagement to be married is not a license for premarital sex. Many engaged couples have believed the opposite and have paid a high price for their naivety.

Approximately "fifty percent of the people who get married have been engaged at least once before," according to Tim Stafford. The obvious corollary to this statistic is painful but true. That is: engaged couples do break up.

Because the engagement period is a time of impermanence, characterized by uncertainty and the tenuous working toward a lifelong commitment, it would be foolhardy to engage in premarital sex. To have sexual relations during this fragile period would be like a child secretly opening his Christmas gifts on December 22, says Walter Trobisch. "Imagine," says Trobisch, "that your father wants to surprise you with a bicycle for Christmas. He hides it carefully. But you take it secretly out of the hiding place and try it out. Then on Christmas Day you have to act as if you are surprised and joyful, but the holiday is colorless and empty" (*I Loved a Girl*).

Perhaps this is why God ordained the institution of marriage and the wedding ceremony. The Lord knows that many times private promises are nothing more than hollow, meaningless words, until they are proclaimed publicly and backed up by a commitment of our lives.

Once Means Forever. With tears in his eyes, Tim shared an insight concerning male-female relationships that I have felt compelled to share wherever I have discussed this subject.

"You know, Ken," he haltingly told me, "there really *is* something about sex that binds two people together. A man and a woman who have shared such intimate oneness were never intended to be separated."

A couple cannot have sex together and then casually walk away as if nothing has happened, as though it were "business as usual" between them. For the rest of your life, anytime you see that person with whom you have been intimate, you will be reminded that something of deep, spiritual significance has been transacted between the two of you. You may try to repress this knowledge by allowing feelings of hatred, bitterness, or revenge toward your partner, or by wallowing in self-pity and self-imposed rejection, but the inescapable truth will always be there, seething just below the surface in your subconsciousness.

Premarital Sex: Hot It's Not!

I know that is not what you have been hearing in the locker room, or what you have been reading in a lot of current literature, or what you have surmised from watching television. The message constantly surrounds us: "Premarital sex is the greatest thing in the world! It's almost like being in heaven!"

Unfortunately, for many unmarried singles who have fallen victim to these lies, their experiences sound a lot more like tales out of hell than bits of heaven.

"Bill told me that everything was going to be wonderful," a naive fifteen-year-old sobbed. "He said I would feel terrific, and it would be the most exciting experience of my life. Well, it wasn't! I was scared to death, and he hurt me so badly, I hope I never have to go through that again!"

Too bad for her. Her first sexual encounter was a negative experience. Now it is going to take a lot of time to overcome the repercussions of her mistake.

One of the few good impacts the Sexual Revolution has had upon society is that people discuss sex much more openly nowadays. Consequently, a loud voice is being heard with greater frequency. People are saying, "Hey, my first attempt at sex wasn't all that it was cracked up to be! To tell you the truth, it was pretty crummy!"

These statements and many others like them are being heard from married and unmarried sex partners alike. How can you account for these unusual revelations?

Part of the blame must be placed on your own trusting naivety concerning sexual matters. Many of you have been hyped into believing a lie. It goes something like this: "On your wedding night [or on the occasion of your first encounter], you will experience fireworks, flashing lights, marching bands, and who knows what other wonderful, thrilling, convulsively ecstatic sensations that are sure to overwhelm you the first time you make love."

Hardly anybody has ever told you that your first encounter might be a real "downer," that it might be one of the most fearful, nerveracking, frustrating experiences of your life! Yet that is precisely what many people have undergone.

One of the questions included in a recent survey asked girls who had engaged in premarital sex to evaluate their reactions by listing descriptive words about their initial sexual experience. Most of the girls used words like *guilty, afraid, embarrassed,* and *worried.* That's quite a difference from "fireworks and marching bands"!

Most married couples will admit that the first night of their honeymoon, though perhaps romantically exquisite, was not sexually ideal. Why? Because great sex takes much more than two sweaty bodies locked in an embrace. It takes time, patience, adjustments, and most of all, unconditional love.

Future Block. Since these essential ingredients are missing, premarital sex can create some formidable barriers to your future sexual satisfaction. A poor initiation into what God intended to be a beautiful aspect of marriage causes many a single person who indulges in forbidden fruit to develop a bitter taste for the whole idea of sex. This is especially true of girls, but guys are equally susceptible. Isn't that ironic? The very activity which we are led to believe will improve our sexual prowess, holds the potential to plunge us into physical or emotional impotence, or both!

Dr. Herbert Miles has emphatically stated:

> Premarital sex relations have a detrimental effect upon the attitudes and ideas of youth about the nature of sex. Before premarital experimentation, young people usually think of sex as something wonderful to be anticipated.... But premarital experimentation often destroys this wholesome ap-

proach. First sexual experiences are notoriously unsuccessful. Also, they are intensely impressive. Usually, they are one-sided affairs in which the girl reluctantly yields while the boy awkwardly and hastily satisfies his own selfish desires. . . . The experience is neither satisfying nor pleasant to the girl. . . . Often the boy senses her disappointment and secretly feels that he is not a real man. Guilt feelings make them both miserable for days and sometimes for years. Actually, there is nothing wrong sexually with either the girl or the boy. Their problem is simply that two people just cannot find sexual fulfillment in such a situation.

Sexual Understanding Before Marriage

You are probably chuckling to yourself right now, "Ho, ho! That guy sure doesn't know me! Nothing in this world could ever turn me off sex! Bad sex, good sex, any kind of sex—I'll take it!"

Unfortunately, you are wrong. While premarital sex isn't all that hot, it is still hot enough to burn you, and it will if you let it. Premarital sex leaves searing marks and oftentimes these marks mar a person for life.

Guilt and the Deep Freeze. A far more common and much more detrimental attitude that oftentimes develops as a result of premarital sex is that of guilt. Believe it or not, guilt as a result of sexual misbehavior *before* you are married can cause you to have a lousy sex life *after* you are married!

R. C. Sproul is convinced that many common sexual problems in marriage can be directly traced to premarital experiences. Says Sproul:

One question I frequently ask men who complain to me about their wives' frigidity is, "Did you have sexual relations with your wife before you were married?" . . . In every case where I have asked this question, the man has answered in the affirmative. Then I ask the next question: "Would you say that your wife was more or less responsive to you sexually before you were married?" Again, in every case where I have asked this question, the man has replied quite emphatically that his wife was indeed more responsive before they were married.

Perhaps it was because sex was a novelty for her that now has grown dull. Perhaps the fact that sex was forbidden made it more exciting for her. Or it could be for a host of other reasons. But one explanation should be given weighty consideration. Perhaps the woman feels so guilty about her loss of virginity before marriage that she is now suffering the paralyzing effects of that guilt.

The woman may experience guilt and feel resentment toward the husband, unconsciously punishing him by withholding herself from complete involvement. Or the woman may have difficulty in giving herself to the man who offended her (even if *she* encouraged him to sleep with her). Another factor may be that the woman felt "bound" to the man once she slept with him and she would not have married him if they had not had intercourse. The woman may feel "trapped" in marriage.

Discovering the Intimate Marriage

While public acknowledgment of guilt feelings among guys who had sex before marriage is less widespread, this does not mean that men are escaping premarital affairs unscathed. Tim and Bev La-Haye, in their book *The Act of Marriage,* report that guilt, as a result of premarital sex, is one of the major reasons for sexual impotence among men. Isn't that sad? Because of sexual escapades in their pasts with women whom they obviously did not love, many men cannot now function properly with the woman they do love!

Poor Attitude and Lousy Technique. Two other areas of a guy's future sex life are profoundly affected by sex before marriage. Those areas involve his attitude and his technique.

Let's talk frankly about this. Much of premarital sexual activity usually takes place in a tense, hurried atmosphere, such as a drive-in movie, or while your mom and dad are out of the house for a few hours, or at your guy's or girl's apartment. Because of the surrounding conditions, you program into your mind that sex must be a furtive, rushed, secretive activity. Often during premarital sexual affairs, the attitude is one of "Let's hurry up before we get caught!"

These circumstances and attitudes are exactly opposite of those so necessary for good sexual relations within marriage. In order to completely enjoy sex, there must be an atmosphere of unhurried privacy, freedom to express yourself, lack of fear or resistance, a relaxed attitude mentally and physically, perfect trust, and total acceptance of your partner. Premarital sex simply does not provide that atmosphere.

Consequently, most men who have premarital experiences program into their psychological systems a lot of ideas and actions that are counterproductive to good sex within marriage.

A young wife came to my office for counseling. "Joey doesn't know how to make love," she complained. "He knows how to have sex, but he doesn't know how to make love. He thinks a good sex life is riding through our bedroom like the Lone Ranger, in a cloud of dust and a flurry of action. Bang! Crash! Boom! It's over, and he's gone. He doesn't understand that I need him to hold me, to touch me, to make me feel like a woman, not just a machine he uses for sexual release."

When I talked to Joey, I delicately broached his wife's complaint. Eventually, we got around to discussing his premarital sexual activity, as it related to their marriage.

"I had sex with a number of girls, including my wife, before I got married," he admitted. "A lot of my experience took place in parked cars. Sometimes I would go to a girl's home, but even then I had to get home before the night was over. I guess I just figured sex had to be a quick fling."

Joey and his wife are now conscientiously working at the process of reversing a lot of the programming in their "sexual computers." How much better off they would have been if they had controlled themselves and abstained from sex until they were married!

8

Heartbreakers

Having discussed some of the psychological and spiritual reasons for abstaining from sex until you are married, let's move on to three time-honored reasons for eschewing premarital sex. They are valid today. These "three heartbreakers" are *pregnancy, venereal disease,* and *guilt.*

Baby Blues

In past years, our society largely opposed premarital sex, because it often resulted in premarital pregnancies. Nowadays, we have tended to minimize that threat because of sex education, birth control, and casual abortion. Yet, despite all our knowledge and scientific breakthroughs, single girls still get pregnant and give birth to unwanted children—or abort them, compounding guilt and sin.

Furthermore, while the Pill helped usher in an era of sexual looseness, many young people do not utilize birth-control devices. They are, therefore, tossed about on a sea of sensuality.

According to a study by Johns Hopkins professors Melvin Zelnik and John F. Kantner:

Nearly 50 percent of the nation's 10.3 million young women age 15 to 19 have had premarital sex.... One disturbing consequence of this advanced sexuality is that teen-age pregnancies are epidemic: one million teen-age girls—one out of every ten—get pregnant each year. Statistics in a 1977 study show that 600,000 unwed teen-agers were giving birth each year, with the sharpest increase among those under 14.

"The Games Teen-agers Play,"
Newsweek, September 1, 1980

Now, would you please read that last paragraph again and let those figures sink into your brain for a moment?

Think of it! One out of two girls between the ages of fifteen and nineteen in our country has engaged in premarital sex! One girl out of every ten within the same age group got pregnant! Furthermore, young girls under fourteen years of age are getting pregnant at a staggering rate! With the age for "legal cohabitation" being dropped in many states (thirteen years of age in some states!), this phenomenon is likely to increase even more.

The undeniable and unfortunate fact remains: unwed young women are getting pregnant with more frequency than ever. Of course, unwed mothers are not restricted to the category of teen-agers. Young women in their twenties and thirties get pregnant without husbands, too. Nor is this dilemma unknown within Christian circles. Sad to say, far more Christian families than we would care to admit have been forced to suffer through the emotional and spiritual drain of an illegitimate pregnancy.

"Mom, I'm pregnant," are about the most devastating words that parents of an unmarried daughter can ever hear. If you have ever been involved with a family in which these words have been spoken, you know what a nightmare it can be.

There are no easy answers, no instant remedies, for a premarital pregnancy. Any way you look at it, there are some terribly tough decisions to be made. No matter how sensitively and delicately the situation is handled, somebody (and usually more than one somebody) is going to sustain injury and pain that is not likely to disappear quickly.

When a premarital pregnancy occurs, there are basically only four options.

(1) *A Shotgun Wedding*. Option number one is that of a quick marriage, sometimes known as a "shotgun wedding." In this situation, a couple goes ahead and plans a quick wedding, usually organized before the girl begins "to show." Sometimes this is done simply to "give the baby a name." In other situations, the quick wedding is announced in order to save the couple and their families from public embarrassment. However, quick weddings, planned as a result of an unplanned pregnancy, run an enormously high risk of resulting in a quick, unplanned divorce.

Yes, I know some couples that "had to get married" who are happy with their marriages. On the other hand, a lot of them are not. Many of these couples have endured a cruel caricature of marriage since their wedding day. For him, his marriage symbolizes an entrapment and a loss of freedom. For her, it symbolizes an imposition upon her life and the burden of a child before she was ready. Of course, the born loser in this situation is the innocent, unsuspecting baby, who often becomes the victim of resentment and mistreatment by the bitter parents.

Even if a quick wedding is agreeable to all parties, and the couple involved is deeply in love, it is still sort of sad. The biggest day in a girl's life seems stained by murmurings, snickerings, and innuendos. Her beautiful, white gown is more a symbol of derision than one of expectant purity.

(2) *Abortion*. With disturbing frequency, abortion is being used as an alternative among pregnant young women. Many times this appears to be the easiest way out in comparison to the horror of facing parents, friends, and the knowing looks of others in the community. Saving face, no matter what the cost, is the crucial issue.

A few years ago, I was privileged to be the main speaker for the National Church of God Youth Workshop in Findlay, Ohio. In order to get some feedback from the young adults to whom I was speaking and to make myself more accessible to them, each afternoon I located a shady spot in the oak grove and sat down. There, I'd wait . . . just in case any of the guys or girls wanted to talk to me. Every day they'd come, sometimes ten, sometimes twenty, sometimes as many as fifty. We discussed anything on their minds—sex, abortion, masturbation, incest, and a host of related topics.

One day, following such a session, I noticed an innocent-looking fellow lingering a little longer than the others. When he finally was alone with me, he opened up. "I never thought I would be a part of such a thing," he said quietly. "But when Martha became pregnant, I didn't know what else to do. We weren't ready for marriage, especially under those circumstances. And we certainly weren't ready to raise a child . . . I mean, hey, man, we were only eighteen ourselves!

"I was never so scared in all my life. I couldn't even imagine having to face Martha's parents or mine. They all thought we were such a lovely Christian couple. And her dad is a preacher!

"I read about this place in Detroit that would do the job, no questions asked, so I suggested it to Martha. At first, she was horrified to even think about it. We both thought that abortion was one of the cruelest things our modern age has devised. Of course, that was before *we* were faced with a pregnancy ourselves. Think about it . . . we killed an unborn child just to save our reputations."

(3) *You and Me, Baby!* A third possible course of action when an unmarried girl finds herself pregnant is that of having the baby and raising a child as a single parent. Whether the unmarried woman is living at home with her parents or on her own with her child, there are myriad complications with this option.

The mother is often robbed of any meaningful interaction with other young people her own age. Naturally, her first responsibility must be to her baby, and babies take time; lots of it! Very little time is left for socializing, either with old friends or to establish new friendships.

Dating, for the single mother, although not impossible, is certainly not as simple a process as it was before the birth of her child. Most guys simply do not like the idea of a "ready-made" family.

That sounds cruel and insensitive, and true, there are exceptions. Still, most men are reluctant to ask out a woman who has a child but has not had a husband.

(4) *Adoption.* Adoption is another possible alternative, although it is still fraught with difficulties. For some girls, much of the guilt and fear associated with abortion is present in an adoption, though not, perhaps, to such an intense degree. Still, in some ways an adoption is even more difficult for a young mother to handle. For one thing, there must be an admittance of guilt and an enlistment of aid. To many, this, in itself, makes abortion look more attractive.

Furthermore, the public spectacle, embarrassment, and the downright inconveniences of dropping out of school or work to have a baby are heightened and more prolonged. This time element is often a very hard aspect of adoption with which an unmarried mom must deal. The expectant mother must carry her child the full nine-month gestation period. When the child has been a part of her for such a long period of time, it is difficult for many a mother to give her baby away.

On the positive side of adoption, at least the child will be afforded the opportunity to grow up in a "normal" home environment, hopefully with loving, understanding, parents who will sensitively help the child deal with his adoption at the right time and under the right circumstances. Ideally, it would be desirable to work with a Christian adoption agency and the child be placed in a genuinely Christian environment in which Jesus Christ would be the center.

Let's face it! There simply is no such thing as a "good" solution to a pregnancy that occurs before a couple is married! No matter how it is handled, there will be pain, guilt, and tears. The beautiful, anticipated event of giving birth within a marriage, in which two people are totally committed to each other and joyfully looking forward to raising their family—well, it just isn't there. The premarital birth is something to be "dealt with" rather than to be experienced by the couple, family, and friends.

V.D.—Very Dangerous

A few years ago, the U.S. Department of Health, Education, and Welfare branded venereal disease the number one health hazard in the nation today for persons under twenty-four years of age. Did you catch that? Diseases directly related to promiscuity are more dangerous to the health of young adults than are drugs, booze, or even auto accidents!

Venereal disease assumes many different forms, but most all V.D. is transmitted through sexual intercourse. The most prevalent of all venereal diseases is gonorrhea.

Another well-known type of venereal disease is syphilis. While it is no longer as common as gonorrhea, it is more serious. Untreated syphilis can kill you! Syphilis is highly contagious and can be transmitted not only through direct sexual contact, but through any break in the skin.

In both syphilis and gonorrhea, even without medication, the symptoms will usually begin to disappear after a few weeks. However, the disease is not gone; it is still growing ever more serious. During this time, the infected person may show virtually no outward signs of the disease, and even live under the delusion that the affliction has gone away.

If an individual does not receive medical treatment and allows venereal disease to run its course, the consequences may affect the skin, muscles, digestive organs, liver, lungs, eyes, glands, and even the heart and brain.

Does all of this sound frightening? It should! Venereal disease can destroy your life! Flagrant promiscuity is not necessary to contract the disease. Even one sexual experience with an infected person can pass the disease on to you! Granted, penicillin and other antibiotics have been used successfully to treat V.D. *once a person knows he or she has been infected.* Two alarming facts, however, are reason for heightened concern.

One, V.D. is rapidly increasing in frequency among teenagers and those in the preteen years as previously stated in *Newsweek*.

Second, new strains and variations of the diseases now exist that are not curable by any of the formerly effective remedies. Modern-day promiscuous behavior has resulted in antibiotic-resistant venereal diseases for which *there are no known cures*.

One such frightening type of V.D. is known as "herpes." At this writing, it cannot be cured. Like advanced syphilis, its acute symptoms keep reoccurring, time and again. "Herpes can be life-threatening. The incidence of cervical cancer is four times higher among women with herpes than it is among those free of the disease. . . . Even in mild cases, the psychological effects can be devastating. The shame and fear make men impotent and wreck marriages . . ." (*Newsweek*, April 12, 1982).

One of the most bizarre sexually-linked diseases to appear recently is AIDS, acquired immune deficiency syndrome. AIDS is, at present, an elusive mystery killer. Nobody knows what causes it, how to prevent it, or how to cure it. "So far 6,517 cases of AIDS have been reported to the Centers for Disease Control in Atlanta. . . . Nearly half the victims have died, although the ultimate mortality rate may be 90 percent or higher" (*Time*, November 5, 1984).

Medical authorities and members of the scientific community are throwing up their hands in despair, wondering how a halt can be put to these infectious mystery diseases and to the epidemic proportions of V.D.

One way might be to get back to what God said about keeping sex within the boundaries of marriage. In other words, don't have premarital sex, extramarital sex, or homosexual sex, and you will have little worry about catching a sexually transmissible disease.

9

Terms of Endearment

You've sinned. Right? I have too. So has your Mom and Dad, your preacher or priest, and your best friend. Think of the best-living person you know. He or she has sinned too! In fact, the Bible says, "all have sinned and fall short of the glory of God ..." (Romans 3:23).

Moreover, virtually everyone has sinned in the area of sex. If we are going to get anywhere, we might as well be honest. We have *all* sinned in this area at one time or another!

The degree of sin is not the important question. Whether you are guilty of lusting in your heart, improper talk, dirty thoughts, petting, premarital sex, adultery, abortion, homosexuality, or any other type of sexual misconduct, it is still sin, and you are guilty, unless you have been forgiven by God. There is no such thing as a "big sin" or a "little sin" in God's Book. The angels don't sit in heaven keeping score: "Let's see, that's three black marks against Mary for lustful thoughts; ten each against George and Beth for heavy petting. Oh, watch out! That's a big one hundred for Carl and Janice!"

It doesn't work that way. In God's Book, sin is sin, and all sin is of equal repulsiveness to Him. Every sin carries with it the potential to ruin your life now and to destroy your relationship with God forever.

The fact that everybody else is bogged down by the same mess doesn't lessen the burden or relieve the pangs of guilt. Wouldn't you think the universality of sexual sin would make it easier to excuse? (That's what secular society says.)

Rx for Relieving Guilt

The remedy to guilt resulting from sexual sin does not lie in a vain attempt to forget our pasts. The remedy to guilt lies in a personal relationship with Jesus Christ, in receiving His forgiveness and transforming power in your life!

Listen to this:

> But now God has shown us a different way to heaven—not by "being good enough" and trying to keep his laws, but by a new way (though not new, really, for the Scriptures told about it long ago). Now God says he will accept and acquit us—declare us "not guilty"—if we trust Jesus Christ to take away our sins. And we all can be saved in this same way, by coming to Christ, no matter who we are or what we have been like.
>
> Romans 3:21, 22 TLB

If there was no other reason for becoming a Christian, the forgiveness and release from guilt one experiences when he meets Jesus would be rationale enough to make such a commitment!

If you are already a Christian, but have fallen victim to sexual misconduct or any other sin, don't ignore it! Don't try to lay the blame on someone or something else. You need cleansing and forgiveness just as much as the person who has never met Jesus.

Admit not only what you have done, but why you have done it. Sometimes, the "why" of our sin is difficult to understand, but if we trace our motives far enough, many times we will discover a basic root of selfishness. The outward actions are manifestations of the inward sin of self-gratification.

True Confessions

When we "confess" our sins to God, we are not simply to rattle off a list of our infractions of His Word, say, "Amen," and be done with it. When we confess, we are to say the same thing about our sin as God says about it. Say something like, "Yes, God. I agree with You. That sexual sin was wrong. It was grounded in my own selfish lust. I acted in disobedience to Your Word and Your will for my life. I am truly sorry. I ask You to cleanse my heart and forgive me."

Notice: this sort of confession requires a repentant attitude. It will do you no good whatsoever to confess your sin, unless you are willing to turn away from it. Otherwise, you are wasting your time. Your prayers will not go any higher than the ceiling.

One youth adviser told me, "Ken, I am absolutely appalled at the large number of Christian kids who have sex outside of marriage, and then pray that God won't let them get pregnant!" Let's not fool ourselves! God's forgiveness is readily available to all who will honestly approach Him with a contrite attitude. When we genuinely repent of our sin, He genuinely forgives. But, God will not tolerate our trifling.

It's a Tough Turn. Turning away from sexual sin seems almost impossible. Sexual sins seem almost addictive. Though the way may be difficult, it is not futile. Furthermore, it is not perfection in performance that God requires. He seeks an attitude of willingness— willingness to let Christ help you to turn away from your sin. God will even meet you one step closer. If you are not willing to be delivered, but are "willing to be made willing," He can work in you and lead you out of the bondage of sin. This willingness to be changed is an indispensable ingredient of repentance and confession.

Forgiveness Comes in Threes

Josh McDowell points out in *Givers, Takers* that we need to seek forgiveness on three levels. We must seek the forgiveness of *God, ourselves,* and *others.*

Seeking God's Forgiveness. Many scriptural passages emphasize God's tremendous capacity for forgiveness. Here are just a few:

". . . The blood of Jesus His son cleanses us from *all* sin" (1 John 1:7). Can God forgive me of those horrible sins that I don't even like to remember, those that have been suppressed in my subconscious for years? Yes! Yes! He can! There is no stain so deep that the blood of Jesus cannot cleanse it!

Jeremiah 31:34 states, ". . . I will forgive their iniquity, and their sins I will remember no more." God is not only willing to forgive you of your past, He is willing to forget that your sins ever happened! To Him, it is as though the sin never occurred!

Forgive Yourself. Forgiving oneself is not always so easy. This is especially true in sexual sin, because our haunting conscience screams, "I have violated myself!"

Still, if you have honestly confessed and repented of your sin before God, He has forgiven you. It is foolish not to forgive yourself! Furthermore, it is an insult against Jesus if you do not forgive yourself. For you to continue to carry the load of guilt and shame He died to remove is to say, in effect, "Jesus, your life and death were not good enough to remove my sin. Surely, I must make a greater sacrifice to atone for my sins."

We need to label this attitude for what it really is—self-righteousness, perhaps the most subtle of sins, yet just as offensive to God. The idea that we can, somehow or other, make up for the fact that we have sinned is unbiblical.

Avoid rehashing the past. You want to remember the lessons you learned through your negative experiences, but don't allow yourself to live in the past. Stand tall in the confidence that the Creator of the universe has declared you "not guilty." You are free! Now, get up and go on living a life that exemplifies the liberty you have found in Jesus!

You May Be the Forgiver—or the Forgivee. The third aspect of forgiveness requires that you be reconciled with others. This means that you must forgive someone for wronging you. On the other hand, it may demand that you go to someone and ask them to forgive you for the hurt you have caused them. Both aspects of forgiveness are difficult, and you will need God's help to carry them out.

To forgive someone who has used you sexually is tough love. It takes a lot of prayer, a lot of will, and a mature consciousness of the forgiveness God has bestowed upon you. Jesus told His disciples, "If you forgive men their transgressions, your heavenly Father will forgive you. But if you do not forgive men, then your Father will not forgive your transgressions" (Matthew 6:14, 15).

A forgiving attitude toward others is a must, if we are to grow spiritually ourselves. If someone has sinned against you, forgive them. For God's glory, for their sake, and for your own spiritual health, forgive them!

Jesus also taught that if we have harmed someone else, we should go to that person and make things right, as far as possible. He said:

> "If therefore you are presenting your offering at the altar, and there remember that your brother has something against you, leave your offering there before the altar, and go your way; first be reconciled to your brother, and then come and present your offering."
>
> Matthew 5:23, 24

Seeking Forgiveness of Sexual Sin. This command of Jesus is valid and necessary for every type of social sin, but it is especially important for those who have been guilty of sexual sin. There are, however, some problems unique to the person who seeks the forgiveness of another regarding sexual misconduct.

For example, if you steal another person's money, you can apologize, ask forgiveness, and return the money. However, if you rob someone of his or her virginity, or use someone as a means of selfish gratification, how can you possibly make restitution? *You can't.* You cannot give back a person's virginity or dignity. You cannot erase the memories of your intimacy. You can only apologize as best you are able and ask for your partner's forgiveness. In doing so, be careful that you do not give the other person the impression that you are blaming him/her for your failure. Be certain the person understands that you are seeking forgiveness; you are not trying to project your guilt onto someone else's shoulders.

When seeking forgiveness for past sexual activities, don't use the pronoun *we* unless you must. Make this sort of statement: "I was wrong. Since I've met Jesus [or have gotten back into a right relationship with Him], I realize that I was not acting in your best interests or mine. The Lord has shown me that I have been selfish and foolish."

Clarify that God's will has been revealed to you through the Bible. This prevents the offended party from misinterpreting your motives. It lets the person know you are basing your actions on the authoritative source of God's Word, not simply on an emotional whim, as a result of a guilt complex.

Continue along these lines: "I now understand that I have sinned against God, against you, and against myself. I have already asked God for His forgiveness, and I have forgiven myself. Now, I want you to know how sorry I am for my actions in the past. Would you please forgive me?"

It is important that you *ask* for forgiveness. To say you are sorry is merely a statement of fact. To ask forgiveness requires a response from the other person. Forgiveness is theirs to grant or to refuse, but not yours to demand.

Pray with the one you have offended, if possible. Keep your prayers short and to the point. Address your heavenly Father and let Him know that you are grateful for His forgiveness. Thank God for your partner and his or her willingness to forgive you. Ask God for increased ability to go on from here to live according to His will. Be careful that you do not point an accusing finger while you are praying. Whatever else you pray, *don't* pray, "And God, please help my brother [or sister] to see...." You just do your part. Let the Holy Spirit do the convincing of your partner if there remains work to be done.

A Foul Is a Foul. What may seem trivial to one person concerning sexual misconduct may be the source of intense guilt for another. As such, it's a good idea to seek forgiveness no matter how great an offense you and your partner have committed.

Jenny and Andy were classmates at a Christian college. They lived in the same part of the country, so they often rode home together on weekends. On one occasion, Andy casually let his arm slide down the car seat, until it rested softly on Jenny's shoulder. When Jenny shifted slightly, Andy's arm slid off her shoulder and fell across her breast. Immediately, he recoiled and slapped his hand back to the top of the seat.

Jenny, sensing Andy's embarrassment, took his hand in hers. She smiled at him as she pressed it to her lips. They continued to caress each other for the remainder of the trip, a blanket hiding their actions from the view of their fellow passengers. Only for brief moments did Andy or Jenny allow each other to touch what most people would describe as erogenous areas of the body. Still, that was enough to damage their self-images, their impressions of each other, and their spiritual conditions.

Back at school, during a church service, Andy began to feel deeply convicted about his past actions with Jenny. He got down on his knees and prayed for forgiveness. Almost immediately, he felt the Lord instructing him to go and apologize to Jenny.

"But, Lord! She'll probably think I'm nuts for coming to her over such a little thing! I mean ... after all, Lord, this is the twentieth century!" Andy protested.

Andy rose from his knees and turned to leave the church. He glanced back over his shoulder and stopped short in his steps. There, sitting about ten rows back in the room, was Jenny! Her head was bowed, and she was praying softly out loud.

"It's now or never," he sensed the Lord saying to him.

"Er . . . ah . . . ah-hem," Andy began nervously.

Jenny looked up at him, startled by the sound of his voice. There were tears in her eyes.

Andy started again. "Ah, Jenny, would you mind if I talked with you?" His voice sounded weak and raspy.

"No, Andy," she answered sweetly. "I wouldn't mind."

"Well, do you remember when we rode home together?" Andy felt a rush of color storm his face as he asked the question. *How stupid of me!* he thought. *Of course she remembers! It was only a few weeks ago! How could she forget?*

If Jenny thought it was foolish question, her expression didn't show it. She simply answered, "Yes, what about it?"

"Yes, well, some of the things I did weren't too Christian, and I want you to know that I'm sorry, Jenny. I'd like to ask you to forgive me."

"Oh, Andy!" she exclaimed, as she reached out and grabbed both of his hands with hers. Tears were once again flowing down her cheeks. "I was so worried about what you thought of me after that night! I felt dirty all over! I couldn't sleep; I spent the whole night asking God to forgive me. When I came back to school, every time I'd see you, I'd feel guilty. I started to hate you. I'm sorry, Andy. Please forgive me, will you? It was as much my fault as it was yours."

They prayed together, then walked out of the church, clean before God and in a right relationship with each other.

To the casual observer, the indiscretions of Jenny and Andy would seem infinitesimal. To those two young people, however, their sins represented major breaches of God's will for their lives. They could only be free as they found forgiveness in Him and in each other. The same is true for you and me.

To Everything There Is a Season. A question that pops up frequently is, "Ken, do you think we should *always* seek a partner's forgiveness for sexual misconduct?"

My usual answer is, "Usually." In most cases, I recommend that you seek to make past wrongs right. Sometimes it is simply not possible. Perhaps you have lost contact with an injured party, or you are separated by a long distance. In such cases, you might be wise to forego seeking forgiveness until it is possible to hold a face-to-face confrontation, or, at least, a telephone conversation. Never write a letter seeking forgiveness, unless you feel certain the Spirit of God is leading you to do so. A written confession requesting forgiveness might easily come back to haunt you and your former partner, should it ever turn up in the wrong hands.

Sometimes I do not encourage approaching the wounded party. One young man began to feel guilty about a sexual affair he had shared with his best friend's wife. Feeling superspiritual about the entire matter, he gathered the wife and friend together for a time of confession. He ruined both his friendship and the couple's marriage.

While we certainly want to be obedient to our Lord's command, a little common sense, tact, and Spirit-led discretion will go a long way in helping to deal with such sensitive matters.

The secret here, of course, is being able to detect God's clear leading. Generally, we should act on what we already know to be God's will. He has already instructed us to seek forgiveness with the offended party. For those cases in which you are honestly not sure about what would be the best thing to do, here are some suggestions.

If the leading is of the Holy Spirit, it will most likely result in prolonged conviction. He will continue to gently nudge you about the matter until you comply with His wishes. It will not be a passing thought that suddenly occurs to you and quickly disappears. God is not above speaking to you more than once. He wants to reveal His will to you and will repeat His instructions if you do not understand. Don't be afraid to ask God for clarification of His will. He will not get angry with you, not if you are being honest with Him, that is. If you are simply stalling for time, that is a different issue, but if you truthfully want to do right, but aren't sure of His will, He will be more than glad to confirm His Word for you.

Second, if the inclination you are feeling is truly of the Holy

Spirit, *you can count on Him to provide an opportunity for you to seek forgiveness in a discreet manner.* This is not to imply that the Holy Spirit will help you to cover your sin. On the contrary, He is the One who convicts of sin, righteousness, and judgment (John 16:8). Nevertheless, the Spirit of God is not in the business of destroying marriages and reputations or uncovering healed wounds needlessly through the stupidity of a well-meant, but ill-conceived, confession of your past sexual improprieties. If He is instructing you to confess and seek forgiveness, He will also present the opportunity at the right time, in the right place, and under the proper conditions. Trust this area, especially, to His judgment, not your own.

Third, *if there is to be any more public acknowledgment of your sin, be sure to let the Holy Spirit be your guide.* I find it difficult to believe that the Spirit of God would ever lead someone to reveal the name or names of sexual partners, but much to my surprise, I have heard just such misguided revelations during "testimony meetings." Such public confessions are usually quite "fleshly" (in more ways than one!) and are hardly glorifying to our Lord Jesus Christ.

It seems far more usual that the Holy Spirit would lead you to seek out an opportunity for a private consultation with the party you have offended. Once that reconciliation takes place, and forgiveness is realized between both partners and between the individual partners and God, the matter is closed.

10

Keeping the Lid On

A young man listened intently as I spoke to his Penn State fellowship about forgiveness. Afterward, he asked me if we could talk.

"How, Ken?" he implored. "How can a guy and a girl keep themselves pure? It's great to know we are able to be forgiven when we mess up, but how does God expect us to keep the lid on the sexual pressure cooker?"

I have heard that young man's cry echoed by thousands of unmarried men and women, as I have traveled around the country. Many devout Christians are grappling with the difficult problems related to sexuality and singleness.

Temptation Skips No One

It would be nice to think that once we have reached a certain plateau in our spiritual climb, we would be immune from temptation. I have heard several people make such lofty claims.

One man stood up in the middle of a room where I was speaking on this subject and proclaimed adamantly, "Why, I'm not troubled by temptation! I certainly don't have any problems with lust. I am a

Christian! Jesus has delivered me out of that, and I am no longer affected by *sss . . . sss . . . sssss . . .* that!"

Maybe so, but I doubt it.

As a Spirit-filled believer, I agree that the victorious Christian life includes victory over sexual lust and temptation. Nevertheless, no spiritual experience, no new dispensation of God's gracious gifts, no new state of Christian living, no act of God, Himself, is going to prevent you from being tempted. Jesus was tempted; Paul was; I am; and you will be, too!

Temptation Is Not Sin. You can be tempted, though, without having to sin. The sin factor does not enter until a person yields to temptation. While this may be elementary to some who are veterans along the Christian Way, it is often a revelation to others.

Many Christians have acquired the false notion that says, "Boy, if I am really 'spiritual,' I should not still be plagued with these temptations." Actually, nothing could be further from the truth. The devil does not give up his fight simply because you have established a relationship with Jesus Christ. Satan will be trying to pull you down into hell until the very day he and his heinous cohorts are finally destroyed (Revelation 20:10).

The Devil Can't Make You Do It. The question, then, is, "When does sexual temptation turn into sexual lust?" Billy Graham used to say that it is not the first look that is sin, but it is the second look, and the third. . . . Sin begins when we allow our minds to dwell upon that lustful thought, or allow our eyes to linger unduly on that sexually stimulating subject, or permit ourselves to purposely remain in a sexually arousing situation. Then, temptation gives way to lust, which turns into sin, and eventually leads to death (James 1:14, 15).

Because temptation is common to all of us, you cannot pass off the responsibility of resisting temptation to someone else. *You* must flee temptation. God has promised that He will help you. Your heavenly Father, in His permissive will, allows temptations to come your way, but He is never out of touch; He is never out of control.

He "will not allow you to be tempted beyond what you are able, but with the temptation will provide the way of escape also, that you may be able to endure it" (1 Corinthians 10:13).

Nevertheless, it's not enough, when you find yourself in a tight spot, simply to say, "Well, Lord, if You didn't want me to be here, or doing this, You would have gotten me out of this mess!" Notice, the Scripture says God will "provide the way of escape." *You* must take the action to escape the situation.

If you are getting all worked up on the couch at your girl friend's house, I doubt that you are suddenly going to find yourself whisked away in a cloud, plopped down in the driver's seat of your car, headed home. I know the Lord pulled some fantastic maneuvers with Elijah and Philip, but I don't think that is what He has in mind for you.

The Bible says, "Submit therefore to God. Resist the devil and he will flee from you" (James 4:7). There, in a nutshell, is the formula for conquering temptation. First, *submit your life continually to God.* Then, *resist the devil today!* Remember, he is a defeated foe. Jesus beat him at Calvary. Still, you must act upon that victory, claiming authority over Satan, in the name of Jesus, and resisting the devil's attempts to pull you down.

Practical Helps

Some simple steps will help keep you pure sexually, or help regain and maintain your spiritual purity if you have failed.

(1) *Avoid Bad Company.* Paul does not pull any punches when he charges us, "Do not be misled: Bad company corrupts good character" (1 Corinthians 15:33 NIV). Try to take an objective look at the people with whom you spend most of your leisure time. What are their attitudes toward love, sex, marriage, and dating? Where do they spend most of their spare time?

It makes sense that the people you are "hanging out" with are going to have an impact on you. They will influence everything from the way you dress to the way you act, think, and talk. They can influence you positively, helping you to be more of the man or woman God wants you to be; they can influence you negatively, drawing you away from the things of the Lord.

But positive fellowship takes special effort. One of the complaints I often hear is, "There aren't any Christian men or women around here! We have eight or ten in our singles group, and that's about it!" I attended a small church as I was growing up, so I can relate.

Still, you can do what you want to about this problem. Okay, so you only have a few people in your fellowship; surely there are other groups with which you can get together in your area. Most churches have regional get-togethers. Many parachurch organizations have regularly scheduled activities. If there is no action near you, either start some, or go to where the action is!

(2) *Be Careful How You Dress.* A quick glance around your church on Sunday morning will oftentimes reveal that even Christians need a reminder to be cautious concerning their appearance. This admonition used to be leveled only at the female gender. Nowadays, many ladies are pointing accusing fingers at the male sex, as well, regarding immodest apparel.

God wants you to look good! As His children, your personal appearance is an outward reflection of what His Holy Spirit is doing inside you. You need to be ever conscious of the fact that your attire is making a statement. Unfortunately, if you are not careful, the way you look can easily give the impression that you are representing the opposition.

Body Language. Our personal appearance provides the perfect opportunity to transmit sexual signals. In recent years, men, as well as women, have become more blatant at this. Consequently, men, you need to be conscious of the impact your appearance is provoking.

Man of God, if you are strutting around, wearing a shirt unbuttoned to your waist and a pair of form-fitting jeans, or you hit the beach in a bathing suit that barely covers your genitals, you may be emphasizing your manliness, but certainly not your godliness! Modesty and good taste are equally important virtues for women and men.

Still, women hold the upper hand when it comes to sensual appeal. This distinction exists because men are primarily aroused through sight, whereas women are more sensitive to touch. As such, a Christian young woman must always keep in mind the effect her appearance is having on surrounding males.

Melody Green, wife of the late, well-known, Christian musician Keith Green, in an article discussing modesty says:

> It amazes me to see young girls (and even mature women) in church or at outdoor festivals and gatherings, hands uplifted offering praise to God, with their necklines plunging and their skirts slit halfway up their thigh. They don't seem to even think twice about wearing see-through blouses, halter-tops, short-shorts, or tight tee-shirts and pants. Many wear scanty bathing suits or even bikinis while thinking, "It's okay, 'cause I'm swimming." Actually, sometimes it seems to me that many are just looking for an acceptable "Christian" excuse to take it all off!
>
> These women are lost in their own selfish little world, oblivious to their effect on others—not caring at all if they are causing someone to stumble. Many seem innocent to any wrongdoing and appear to have a real excitement and love for the Lord, but all the while, their body is sending out a totally different message. I know! Because ... I have done it ... partly in ignorance, but mostly in rebellion. I would think, "Well, it's not my fault if they can't keep their eyes off me and on the Lord. They just aren't spiritual enough. I like my clothes! Why should I have to change just because they are weak?"

But the Lord said, "Melody, it is your fault. You are causing your brother to stumble. You are responsible. Look at the
way you are dressed ... you ought to be ashamed of yourself."

Last Days Newsletter, No. 5, July-October 1980

Probably no area of a Christian young woman's life holds more
potential for causing her male counterpart to stumble than in her
choice of clothing. This power should never be regarded lightly by
any sincere woman of God.

What Does the Original Designer Say? What looks good in God's
sight and what looks good in the sight of "the world" are often at
divergent poles. God places a premium upon the internal qualities
of a person; the world is often content to package the exterior.

The apostle Peter exhorts Christian women:

> Your beauty should not come from outward adornment, such
> as braided hair and the wearing of gold jewelry and fine
> clothes. Instead, it should be that of your inner self, the un-
> fading beauty of a gentle and quiet spirit, which is of great
> worth in God's sight. For this is the way the holy women of
> the past who put their hope in God used to make themselves
> beautiful. ...
>
> 1 Peter 3:3–5 NIV

Those who place their emphasis on the externals are missing the
primary thrust of the passage. Certainly, a woman of God should
not be dependent upon hairstyles, jewelry, or designer fashions for
her attractiveness. God wants His women to emphasize the inner
qualities of a calm and serene spirit, qualities that are extremely becoming and will not fade away with the passing of time.

Does this mean that a Christian girl should dress like her clothes
were designed by Omar the Tentmaker? Certainly not! A woman's
clothes should be fun for her to wear and attractive to all who see.
Clothes should emphasize her femininity and gracefulness, rather
than the sensual.

One further word needs to be said about dress: God does not have any particular penchant for dull, drab clothing. If you enjoy wearing brackish browns or grizzly grays, go right ahead. But please don't think you are doing God a favor or that you are more "spiritual" for doing so! You can be just as spiritual in hot pink, gorgeous green, or dazzling yellow. Remember, our God is the Creator of all beauty. He is pleased when you use all the colors of His creation to honor Him.

(3) *Guard Your Leisure.* Through the wonders of this technological age, most of you are spending more time doing leisurely things and less time at work. This can be a blessing to you or a curse.

Remember King David? His life and ministry would have been radically different had he kept a closer watch on his leisure time. His sin with Bathsheba might never have happened if David had been fighting on the battlefield, along with his troops.

The same principle is true in your life. You need to keep busy for God; you need to be about your heavenly King's business, and when you are not, you need to guard carefully your leisure.

Personal Battles. In my own life, when I come in from "the road," after a time of ministering, it is then that I need to be especially cautious concerning temptations. I am physically tired, emotionally, and oftentimes, spiritually drained. I am at my lowest ebb after a great concert tour. When I come home in that condition, all I want to do is lie back, rest, and recuperate.

The devil, too, is aware of my depleted condition. He knows that my guard is down, my armor has been taken off for cleaning, shining, refurbishing. He knows that it won't take much to get me to think or act in ways that are foreign to the ways of God's Spirit, and in a manner that, under ordinary circumstances, would be despicable and untenable to me, as well.

It took me several years to discern this subtle stratagem of Satan. When I finally realized what was happening, I initiated a counterattack. If I came home in an exhausted state, I purposely surrounded myself with spiritually uplifting influences. I made it a point to turn off my TV or radio if it was spewing forth negative material that could be used by Satan to pull me down. I sought Christian people, Christian TV programs, Christian music, and other positive input. I would work harder at my own devotional life. I would listen to tapes of the Bible while I was in the shower, getting dressed, or while I was falling asleep at night. If I felt strong pangs of loneliness, I would get in my car and point it in the direction of some Christian fellowship, where I would find others who believed as I do about Jesus' role in our lives.

How Far Is Too Far?

In *Straightforward,* Larry Tomczak described petting as "extremely intimate sex play, yet short of sexual union. Petting behavior may include (either directly or through the clothing) fondling of the girl's breasts, touching and rubbing of one another's genitals (or in the general vicinity), possibly placing bare genitals together but avoiding penetration...."

Petting is not dirty or sinful. It was designed by God to be an integral part of the foreplay leading to sexual intercourse between a husband and wife *in marriage.* That petting leads to sex, we have no doubt. That petting is to be restricted to marriage is an often-ignored law of God.

Paul wrote, "It is good for a man not to touch a woman" (1 Corinthians 7:1). The Greek word translated "touch" can be rendered "to light, to kindle." Any willful activity that is designed to ignite the fires of sexual passion in a person who is not your married partner would, therefore, come under this condemnation.

The Old Testament offers equally stern warnings: "Can a man take fire in his bosom and his clothes not be burned? Or can a man walk on hot coals and his feet not be scorched?" (Proverbs 6:27-29).

The Song of Songs, perhaps the most sexually explicit book in the Bible, says, "Do not arouse love until it pleases" (2:7, 3:5, 8:4). In other words, God is telling us not to begin something that He doesn't want us to carry through to its finish. Before you are married, don't engage in sexually stimulating activities that are intended to culminate in sexual intercourse.

Is Everything Off Limits? Because of such strong scriptural injunctions, genuine Christian singles agree that heavy petting is off limits before marriage. Still, the question inevitably arises, "What physical expressions are permissible in a dating or premarital relationship?" The Christian community has offered a wide variety of answers.

I well remember the dear, saintly gentleman who recounted to my fellow senior collegians the touching story of how he had resisted sexual temptation before marriage. I, too, was sitting on the edge of my seat, as his voice rose to an emotional crescendo in his emphatic conclusion, "And I thank God that never until our honeymoon did my lips touch hers!"

The crowd of students drooped in their seats with one motion, as we tried bravely to suppress our laughter. The girl sitting next to me was not so kind. She blurted out loud, "You've got to be kidding! Where did this guy come from? The Stone Age?"

While the standard of "never kissing before marriage" seems a bit absurd, it is no more ridiculous than the opposite extreme that says, "Anything goes, just as long as a couple does not actually have intercourse."

The intimacy that God has designed to be so wonderful in marriage is certainly there when a couple engages in petting. The blessing of God is not. In fact, says Fritz Ridenour in *The Other Side of Morality,* "If Christ can equate a lustful look with adultery, there seems to be little doubt that heavy petting is to be equated with fornication." As such, all the guilt and condemnation God assesses to those who engage in premarital sex are also designated to those who indulge in petting.

This is something many people fail to understand. Consequently, the practice of petting, and particularly, petting to climax is far more widespread among Christians than most counselors would like to admit—or most parents would believe.

The Age-Old Question. "Okay, as Christians, how far *should* we go?" Guys and girls want to know. Many pastors, counselors, and authors are hesitant to say. Their silence is not necessarily because these "authorities" do not *know* how far is too far or what is right or wrong. They recognize the basic biblical principles that govern premarital sex and petting. However, the specifics of what might be regarded as legitimate and "right" conduct within these boundaries may be different for every couple, each individual, and in every circumstance. This is not to condone "Situation Ethics." It is merely to acknowledge that every Christian is different. Expressions of affection and the responses to such affect people in various ways.

"Sure, sure, sure," a high school senior snipped impatiently. "We understand all that. But isn't there some place where we can draw the line? Isn't there a specific point where we can label our actions as 'okay' and then know after that we are heading for trouble if we go any further?"

All right. At the risk of sounding too liberal to some and too prudish to others, let me give you what I consider to be a viable standard. I believe that any sexually stimulating activity in which a couple engages that goes beyond prolonged kissing is out-of-bounds, counterproductive, and playing with fire. For some, even kissing may be too hot to handle. If so, fine. Set a more stringent standard.

On the other hand, any couple that goes beyond prolonged kissing and enters into petting, caressing, and fondling of obviously erogenous areas of your partner's body, is surely not making a serious attempt to control sexual lust and act in accordance with God's Word. Such couples inevitably go beyond any biblically acceptable limits and mar their relationship with each other and with God.

I like Tim Stafford's comments in *A Love Story:*

For me, kissing expresses love as well as any action short of intercourse can. Anytime I've gotten beyond kissing, I've ended up feeling hot and frustrated. I've felt as though I'd started something I couldn't finish. And torn between the pure sexual desire to go on, and my own responsibility to hold back, I wasn't thinking much about love. At that point it was sex, and the girl could have been any girl. Ending an evening feeling sweaty and unfulfilled is not my picture of the ideal. What good did it do?

Fighting the Fires of Passion. If you are going to implement this "hands-off" policy, you must be hard on yourself and your partner. Do not violate your standard, once it is set. Do not tolerate even minor indiscretions. Remember: the Designer created you in such a manner that once the fires of sexuality are sparked, they quickly turn into blazing forest fires. If you are going to keep things under control, you will need to remain cool and consciously refrain from lighting the fires of passion in your partner.

Who's Responsible Here? A question often raised concerning this matter, is : "In a dating relationship, who is responsible to draw the line on sexually stimulating activity?"

My first response is usually, "Both." The guy and the girl should both work at this. Young woman, if he puts his hands on your body where you know they should not be, gently, but firmly, remove his hands and guide them to wherever you want them to be. You don't have to bite him, slam his hand in the car door, or stick his finger in an electric socket! Just casually slide his hands to a less erotic position. If the guy is any kind of a gentleman, he will get the hint. If he is not a gentleman, what are you doing out with him in the first place?

Girls: don't let your date give you the impression he didn't realize where his hands were. "Golly gee! You mean I was touching you *there!*" If he is a healthy, normal guy, he knows *exactly* where he has been touching you!

Guys: similarly, you need to be aware of any sexual advances that your date might make toward you and take steps to "head her off at the pass." Anyone who thinks that "roaming hands" and other means of enticement are the exclusive property of the male sex has been out of touch with society for a few thousand years!

Women: be sure you realize that just because a guy is a Christian does not mean that he is devoid of sexual desires. Believe it or not, Christian guys respond to sexual stimuli in almost the same way that a nonbeliever does. He is a human being with sexual desires as any other man.

It is a generally accepted medical fact that most guys "turn on" sexually much more quickly than most girls. Women should be aware of this and avoid actions that would tend to submit their guys to sexual heat waves.

A girl complained, "Man, all I was doing was kissing his chest and, suddenly, he was all over me!"

Silly girl!

But let's be straight about this, guys. It is almost a physical impossibility for any woman, no matter how seductive or enticing she is, to *force* you to go further sexually than you want to go. Has it ever occurred to you that even in our warped, so-called sexually permissive society, very few men have ever been raped? Seduced? Certainly. Raped? Hardly. I am not questioning the possibility that a woman may make it extremely convenient for you to go further than you should. Women have powerful sexual desires, too. I am saying, though, that it is not necessary for you to go further than you want to go, than you know you *ought* to go.

Jesus Christ: Social Director

One of the most difficult struggles in the spiritual lives of many Christian singles is the fact that their social lives are so barren. When I suggested to one harried young lady that she become in-

volved in community or church group activities to help fill the social void in her life, she replied hungrily but honestly, "Yes, Ken.
That's very nice, but I want a man!"

If you are dating, the Lordship of Christ assumes that you will
allow Him to choose your dates. No, Jesus won't phone that man or
woman for you, but He will guide your decision-making processes,
if you will allow Him. This means that He will decide who you
should or should not date even within the body of Christ. It is a sad
fact that many Christians have caused great pain to their spiritual
brothers or sisters because of selfish social practices. Bluntly, just
because a person is a Christian does not mean Jesus wants you to
date that person. Perhaps we would be safer to assume that our
Lord wants us to maintain a brother-sister relationship with other
"family members," unless He designates there should be a dating
relationship developed.

That is why I suggest you pray at the beginning of every date.
Your prayer does not have to be a long, drawn-out affair. You don't
have to sing "The Doxology"! (Admittedly, a few girls have told me
their social lives were so dry and empty, when they finally did get in
the car with a real, live date, they *felt* like singing, "Praise God from
whom all blessings flow!")

While such extreme measures are unnecessary, it is important to
commit the occasion to the Lord and ask for His blessing. Say
something like, "Jesus, we thank You for this opportunity to be together, and we want You to be an active participant in our date.
Please bless our conversation and everything that we do. Thank
You, Lord, in advance, for the fabulous time we are going to have
together! *Amen.*"

That's all there is to it. Your prayer can be brief and simple, but
you would be amazed at how effective such prayers are. They are
also excellent at knocking out any lingering ideas that your date
might culminate in sexual activity.

I also suggest that couples pray together at the end of their dates.
Here, again, the prayer can be simple and straightforward. This is

not the time or place to impress your date with your spirituality. You don't have to pray for all the missionaries you know or all the current world crises (though you could, I suppose). Similarly, don't try to pray your way into or out of a good-night kiss! Simply pray and thank the Lord for the evening once more. Let your prayer be one of praise and adoration, as well as thanksgiving.

Try some of the guidelines suggested in this chapter. Nobody said it will be easy but the victory is worth the battle!

11

Mind Over Mental Pollution

In the battle between heaven and hell, the main arena is your *mind!* The devil and his demons know it; the Lord Jesus and His angels know it. When are you and I going to realize it?

Paul recognized that the first place the devil would attempt to stage a counterattack against the Christians at Corinth was their minds. He wrote to them, "But I am afraid, lest as the serpent deceived Eve by his craftiness, your minds should be led astray from the simplicity and purity of devotion to Christ" (2 Corinthians 11:3). Isn't that interesting? The Corinthians were probably having more trouble controlling their sexual lusts than any other of Paul's new converts. Yet Paul was worried about the devil influencing their *minds!* Paul knew where the real battle lines were to be drawn.

Paul instructs us to think positively. He tells us to think about "whatever is true, whatever is honorable, whatever is right, whatever is pure, whatever is lovely, whatever is of good repute, if there is any excellence and if anything worthy of praise, let your mind dwell on these things" (Philippians 4:8).

Paul knew that to win the battle of sexual lust, the Christian must first conquer his thought life. You must guard scrupulously what intake you allow to permeate your mind. Some plain "dos and don'ts" might help.

Thinking Positive and Pure

Choose carefully what movies and television programs you see. You know what excites you sexually. If you are regularly ingesting a diet of sexually explicit movies into your brain, it should come as no surprise that you are having difficulty keeping your thoughts pure and your sexual desires under control. With television programs becoming more erotic, and cable TV systems bringing obscene movies directly into your home, the problem of guarding your mind is getting increasingly difficult. Even the afternoon soap operas, always a bastion of sexual innuendo, are now becoming more blatant in their depicting of bed-hopping sex partners. It is sheer folly to say you are trying to control your sexual appetites and construct a biblical pattern of thinking if you are feeding on such rubbish!

It is also imperative that you carefully screen the literature you read, avoiding especially those magazines and novels that cater to sexual fantasies.

"But I really enjoy the articles in *Playboy* and *Penthouse*," somebody protests. Come *on!* Who do you think you are kidding?

Women cannot afford to be undisciplined in this area, either! Many of the articles in modern-day women's magazines are written from the same hedonistic viewpoint that has catered to male-oriented erotica. Be careful, ladies!

Another type of reading that poses possible dangers, particularly for girls, is the romance novel. Some of these books may extol the virtues of married love and sexual fidelity. On the other hand, many current romance novels tend to glamorize premarital sex, extramarital affairs, and even homosexual affairs. Anything that causes you to fantasize sexually or think in thought patterns that are in direct opposition to God's will can hardly be appropriate in the life of a Christian!

What you hear also has a profound influence on your attitudes about sex. Because of this, you need to use extreme discretion in

your choice of music. A brief listing of some past hits will illustrate
the suggestiveness of some of the music around us.

1. "Sharin' the Night Together"
2. "Nobody Does It Better"
3. "I Want to Kiss You All Over"
4. "Sexual Healing"
5. "Nice Girls (Need It Too)"

Please Pass the Blinders. "Wow! Do you mean that as a Christian
I should never watch movies or TV, read secular literature, or listen
to secular music?" a college-age young woman asked me.

No, I am not your censor. I would rather you rely upon the Holy
Spirit to help you decide what is right or wrong for you. Nevertheless, I do believe that if a Christian is serious about controlling sexual lust, there are some things common sense should tell you.

One guy vociferated piously, "Well, I feel that if a person is a
mature Christian and has his spiritual life together, there is no harm
in keeping up with what is current in the cinemas and on the best-
seller list."

That sounds *real* good. It is ironic that most of the people I have
met who have held to that position were at ebb tide in their own
spiritual lives. They were running on EMPTY, and they were unable
to realize their need. Their spiritual energy had been sapped, and
they were slowly drifting into the sea of spiritual suicide because of
their own tolerance.

Certainly, a mature Christian is free from legalistic, censorious
constraints. Paul cautions us, though, ". . . Happy is he who does
not condemn himself in what he approves" (Romans 14:22).

For example, I don't listen to a large amount of secular pop
music. That may be a treasonable admission from one who makes
his living as a professional musician! Nevertheless, it is true. In my
car, I have over fifty hours of music on cassette tapes. At home, I
have literally hundreds of albums, but in my collection, you would
be extremely hard pressed to find one song with suggestive content.

Do my standards seem too stringent for you? Okay. Set your own. In doing so, do not be deceived. A Christian cannot spend all his time in the playground of the devil and then hope to be of any value on the battlefront for the Lord!

If you truly desire to know what is going on in the world and how it relates to your faith in Christ, there are reviews of music, books, movies, television, and the other arts. Some of these reviews are done from a Christian perspective; many are from a non-Christian view. Evaluate both.

There are also newscasts, magazines, newsletters, and various other informative instruments designed to help keep you knowledgeable of current events and trends. It is possible to remain adequately informed, while you avoid harmful input. Keep the garbage out of your mind but also take positive, offensive action.

A young businessman I knew to be an extremely dedicated Christian confided to me on the beach in Hawaii, "I don't read junk literature; I have never been to a dirty movie in my life, and I don't have a lyrically suggestive album in my entire collection. Yet, I am still losing the battle to lustful thoughts and masturbation. Isn't there anything else I can do?"

I pulled my Bible out from under my beach towel and read aloud, " 'How can a young man keep his way pure? By keeping it according to Thy word. . . . Thy word I have treasured in my heart, that I may not sin against Thee' [Psalms 119:9, 11]. Do you know any other way to stay pure?" I asked him.

He shook his head.

"Neither do I," I said.

Think about it for a moment. What are some of the more common, alternative methods of sexual self-control?

Sublimation Is *Not* the Answer

The most popular method among past generations of Christians has been "sublimation." Sublimation is basically a substitution of mental or physical activity for sexual gratification. In other words, rather than having sex, you are to pour yourself into athletics, hard work, academic study, crossword puzzles, or anything—just as long as it doesn't have sexual overtones! By concentration on other things, you will significantly diminish your sexual desires. Sublimation has been advocated as a viable method of self-control by Billy Graham, the pope, and multitudes of Christian counselors.

There's only one problem with sublimation. *It doesn't work!* If it did, superathletes, construction workers, and Rhodes scholars wouldn't have any problem controlling their sex drives. Obviously, that is not the case.

Sublimation, though helpful in transferring the attention away from your sexual desires, will not alleviate those desires or release the sexual pressures within you. That is why some modern-day Christians are seriously discussing *masturbation* as a credible method of self-control for single Christians.

Varied Viewpoints

Masturbation is the gratification of one's own sexual needs, exclusive of another person. The practice of masturbation seriously divides Christians.

Why this confusion? Possibly nobody has a definite answer because the *Bible doesn't provide one.* The Word of God does not say a word favoring or opposing masturbation.

This conspicuous absence is quickly hailed by many as proof that masturbation is okay. If masturbation is wrong, the argument goes, then why didn't God say so? He was certainly specific enough about adultery, premarital sex, or homosexuality. Surely, if He disapproved of masturbation, it would have been easy for Him to explicitly reveal His feelings. Yet God's Word is silent upon the subject. He has said much more about gossip, lying, pride, jealousy, anger, and drunkenness than He has about masturbation.

Those who favor limited masturbation for men have these reasons for their thinking: The male biological system demands a release of semen. In a normal, healthy man, there is a continuous manufacturing and buildup of semen that must be discharged somehow. The biological "nocturnal emission" is a natural method of sexual release for a man. A nocturnal emission is an automatic ejaculation that occurs during a young man's sleep, following the ordinary buildup of semen. This should not be considered unusual, sinful, or a sign that the person is sexually warped; that he is abnormally dwelling upon dirty thoughts in his sleep. It is simply an ordinary function of the male system, planned and approved by a loving Creator. For some unmarried men, sublimation and nocturnal emissions are sufficient to control their sex drives. Others turn to masturbation.

Many Christians who would condone male masturbation, condemn female masturbation. The reason for this is the lack of biological function within the female that demands a release. The female body does not produce semen. There is no buildup of sexual fluids within her body. This does not mean, however, that there are no emotional buildups within her, demanding to be satisfied, or that she does not experience intense sexual drives.

Arguments Against Masturbation. For both Christian men and Christian women there are some very real reasons for *not* masturbating. *Most notable of these is guilt.* The "world" says masturbation is okay. Some Christian authors, counselors, and even ministers are saying masturbation is okay. Yet, day after day, in cities around the country, I keep meeting men and women who feel guilty, dirty, and sinful because of masturbation.

A lot of guys who come to me about this issue are so guilty and embarrassed, they refuse to even speak specifically about the subject. They usually say, "I have this problem that I just can't conquer." Or, "There's this one sin that keeps coming back again and again." Over the years, I have discovered that, almost inevitably, we are talking about masturbation.

Single girls are even more ambiguous. "I have this habit I wish you'd pray for" often translates, "I am caught between a desire to masturbate and the guilt that results when I do." Surprisingly, women who have been quite open about their immoral sexual escapades with men (or even other women) are often reticent about admitting to masturbation. Masturbation is considered by many single people as the unmentionable sin.

A second argument against masturbation is that *it encourages lustful thoughts.* While it would be admirable to be able to stimulate yourself to the point of sexual release without thinking any lustful thoughts about another person, in reality, that may not be possible for many individuals.

Furthermore, lustful thoughts may become actualized in the form of lustful behavior. A boy may achieve sexual release through masturbation, while fantasizing about his girl friend. Then, the next time he is with his girl friend, there is strong temptation to turn his thoughts into actions.

Perhaps the strongest argument against masturbation is that *sex was never meant to be an individual affair.* God designed your sexuality to be the ultimate, intimate expression of united love between *a husband and a wife.* It is meant to be a joyously shared relationship. Masturbation reduces sex to a matter of powerful drives, momentary pleasure, and self-gratification. It provides the physical release associated with the sex act, but is devoid of the emotional and spiritual union that God intends a married couple to experience through intercourse.

Part III

I Do ... I Think ...
(Single Trials or Wedding Vows?)

12

To Be or Not to Be ... Married, That Is!

"You're next, Kenny Boy!"

Every single person over the age of twenty has been there. You get all dressed up in your Sunday best to go to the wedding of a friend or relative, and what do you get in return?

The Loudmouth. "Hey! What's the matter with you, Ken? You let your brother beat you, didn't you? Heh, heh, heh!"

The Scorekeeper. "Oh, wasn't it a lovely wedding! And how old are you now, Ken? Thirty? And you're not married yet? You'd better hurry up! You're not getting any younger, you know!"

The Comic Sadist. "Hey, come on, Ken! Get with it! Marriage is a three-ring circus! First, there's the engagement ring. Then there's the wedding ring. Then there's suffer-ring! You ought to join the circus, Ken! Ha! Ha!"

Your Old Girl Friend. "Hey, Ken! What are you waiting for? A movie star? More money? I always said you were too picky," as she shuffles her three toddlers from arm to arm.

The Matchmaker. "Do you mean to tell me that you are not married yet? My, oh, my! You're going to make a dandy catch for some lucky girl! You know, my niece . . . yes, the one who lives in Rhode Island, is right about your age, I bet. What a lovely girl she is! Why, I just know the two of you would hit it off great together. She's just your type! Why, she can cook, and she can sew, and she's so pretty, and . . . what did you say your name was again?"

Your Anxious Grandmother. "You'd better hurry up and get married before it's too late!"

Oh, my! It's enough to scare a single guy or girl away from weddings permanently!

It's Okay to Be Single!

The time has come to trumpet the truth. *It's okay to be single!* Did you catch that? It's okay! Really, it is! In fact, both Jesus Christ and the apostle Paul made it clear that for many people, single living may be the preferable alternative.

Unfortunately, secular society as well as the Christian "family of God" have oftentimes given a totally different impression. Many single adults have been battered and browbeaten by proponents of the "Marriage Mystique." The message has been loud and clear: "Every normal boy or girl should grow up, go to school, get a job, get married, settle down, raise a family, and live happily ever after."

A single person, one who has never married, or one who has been married and is single again because of death or divorce, has been made to feel as though he or she is some sort of weirdo from a time warp out in space.

We have been told that if you are single, there must be something wrong with you. Perhaps it is a personality problem. Maybe you are too aggressive or too inhibited. Maybe it's a physical problem. Possibly, you are so ugly or so pretty that members of the opposite sex regard you as an untouchable. Maybe you have an emotional problem. You must be immature, deformed, or *something!*

Maybe you are a sexual pervert. You are either afraid of your own sexuality or, the other extreme, a flirtatious "love 'em and leave 'em" type. Worse still, maybe you have homosexual tendencies. Maybe you are too much of a "homebody," tied to Mommy's apron strings, or unwilling to leave the comfort of Daddy's abode. Maybe you're just too lazy to look for a lover. Surely there must be *something* abnormal about you if you are a single adult!

I know it sounds ridiculous, but society has eyed single adults with suspicion, confusion, and prejudice. Single living has been considered second-rate living. Only recently has our society at large—and the Christian community in particular—come to grips with the fact that it is okay to be single and adult. Prior to this, a single person almost had to have a married person vouch for him. "It's okay, George. He's single but he is an all right sort of guy." A single person had a tough time getting a loan for a car or a home mortgage without the signature of another "more responsible" adult.

Thankfully, though, the Single Stigma is slowly beginning to disappear. Part of the explanation for this phenomenon must lie in sheer numbers alone. More than 60 million people in the USA are opting for a single life-style, according to a "CBS Morning News" series on singleness in America (November 26, 1984).

Many of this new single social set are not single by chance; they have chosen to remain single. True, there are many separated, divorced, and widowed people who are living alone, but on the other hand, of the vast number of single adults in this country, a whopping 50 percent have never been married!

Singleness in America has become socially acceptable. In this respect, as in every other situation, the Bible has been way ahead of us. God said that it was okay to be single a long time ago! The fact that we are just discovering it in the latter moments of the twentieth century simply shows how far we have strayed from (ignored?) His Word.

Two Rather Well-Known Singles

In my own single life, I have often drawn comfort, self-respect, and assurance from the fact that Jesus Christ Himself was a single person. I have no doubt that had our heavenly Father felt it necessary for Jesus to have been married in order to truly exemplify the model life, He would have provided a mate for His Son. However, He didn't. The implications are obvious. Marriage was not a requirement for complete, holy, pure living. Jesus did not need to be married in order to fulfill the ultimate purposes for His life.

Neither did the apostle Paul find marriage a prerequisite to meaningful living. As far as we know, Paul was not married. Perhaps that is one reason why the apostle was one of the most prolific writers in the New Testament. He simply had more time available for writing!

While both Jesus and Paul always spoke highly and respectfully of the marriage relationship, neither of them regarded a person's marital status as something to be envied or despised. The uppermost issue to them was whether or not a person was *rightly related to the Father.*

Should You Get Married?

Pray for the answer to this question: "Father, I know marriage is Your plan for most people, but should I be married? How can I best serve You, married or single? How can You get more glory from my life?"

Until a person receives an affirmative answer to the question "Should I be married?" it is extremely unsafe to proceed in the matter of mate selection.

What Did Jesus, a Bachelor, Say About Marriage and Singleness?

Jesus took the matter of marriage very seriously. In Jesus' eyes, marriage was a permanent commitment. Divorce was not a live option. That is why He emphasized that marriage should never be entered into lightly or for the wrong reasons.

Furthermore, Jesus made it clear that marriage is not for everyone. One passage of Scripture (Matthew 19:3–12) illustrates both of the above attitudes of our Lord.

Among the Jews of that day, there were differing opinions concerning divorce. Some said that divorce was only permissible in a situation in which adultery could be proven to have occurred. Others said that a man could divorce his wife for practically any reason at all!

At first, Jesus avoided taking sides in the debate. He simply restated the Old Testament definition of marriage and reminded His questioners that once a couple was married, they became one flesh and were therefore inseparable.

The Pharisees persisted, "Why then did Moses command to give her a certificate and divorce her?" (19:7).

Jesus answered them with two powerful verbal blasts to the midsection. "He said to them, 'Because of your hardness of heart, Moses permitted you to divorce your wives; but from the beginning it has not been this way. And I say to you, whoever divorces his wife, except for immorality, and marries another commits adultery' " (19:8, 9).

While the Pharisees were still reeling from the attack on their self-righteousness (Hardness of heart? Who? Me?), the disciples of Jesus were trying to put it all together in their own minds. His radical view of divorce must have stunned even them. All they could say was, "If the relationship of the man with his wife is like this, it is better not to marry" (19:10).

Can't you almost see the disciples' faces as they began to realize the implications of Christ's words?

"Wow, Lord! What if I marry the wrong person? If adultery is the only permissible grounds for divorce, and adultery is a sin punishable by death under Jewish law, I'd be better off never to get married in the first place than to marry the wrong person and be trapped!"

What went through their minds we don't know for certain. We do know that the disciples saw clearly the permanence of the marriage union, with its potential for blessing or bondage.

Jesus did not refute His disciples' conclusions. He simply expanded them. He answered them, " 'Not all men can accept this statement, but only those to whom it has been given. . . . He who is able to accept this, let him accept it' " (Matthew 19:11, 12).

What was Jesus saying? Basically, He was agreeing with the disciples' deduction that for some men, it would be better that they remain single rather than to marry. Jesus recognized the potential for greater, unhindered service to God that was possible because of single living. He was quick to qualify that principle, though, by reminding us that only those to whom God has given an ability to function as a single person are equipped for this special life-style.

Jesus was not saying that to serve Him more fully, one must live a life of celibacy. He did not command anyone to be single. Neither did He demand marriage of His disciples. He perceived the possibilities and the drawbacks of both. We certainly should do the same.

Paul's Prescription

The most elaborate discussion of singleness versus marriage in the New Testament came not from the lips of Jesus, but from the pen of Paul. In 1 Corinthians 7, Paul tells us ". . . it is good for a man not to touch a woman" (7:1). The apostle's words, "to touch a woman," can easily be paraphrased, "to have sexual intercourse." The idea of marriage is implicit here. In other words, Paul is saying that it would be good for a guy to remain single.

Nevertheless, Paul, like Jesus, was a realist. Jesus said, "Not everyone can accept this." Paul is saying, "It would be nice; I would prefer that you guys refrain from marriage and sexual contact, but I know that just isn't feasible for most of you."

He goes on, "But because of immoralities, let each man have his own wife, and let each woman have her own husband" (7:2). Paul realized the incredible pressures from sexual temptations that surround single people in a sensual society. Corinth at that time was similar to our society today. It was a sex-saturated society. As such, single Christians who were trying to live holy lives were having a tough time of it. Better, perhaps, that they go ahead and marry. At least then they could have an acceptable outlet for their sexual desires.

Paul is not saying that sex is the *only* reason to get married or even one of the best reasons to get married. Remember, it is this same apostle who gives us the high and holy view of marriage explained in Ephesians 5:22,–33, one of the most exalted passages concerning marriage in Scripture.

A wedding is not a cure-all for sexual lust or temptation. Just ask anyone who is married! If lustful thoughts or actions have plagued you while single, they will probably continue even in the marriage relationship. Paul does say, though, that marriage may be a definite help in self-control.

The apostle continues in First Corinthians, "Yet I wish that all men were even as I myself am. However, each man has his own gift from God, one in this manner, and another in that" (7:7).

It is interesting that the man who had more to say about "gifts from the Lord" than any other writer in Scripture refers to marriage and singleness as a *gift*. Surely, a good wife or husband from the Lord is a treasured gift. However, don't let it escape your notice that Paul also calls singleness a gift!

Most of us tend to think that to live unmarried would be a cross to bear, rather than a gift from God. Still, we dare not ignore the fact that for certain people, singleness would be even more desirable and beneficial than marriage.

Like all other valid gifts, this gift must come from God in order to be used properly and to function effectively within the body of Christ. This gift cannot be bestowed by friends, family, your minister, or other sincere Christians. The gift should not be self-imposed, either. This gift of singleness must come from God or not at all!

Why Remain Single?

It is obvious that the great apostle leans toward single Christian living. Why? With marriage being the wonderful relationship that it is, why would Paul wish that you could all remain single? At least three reasons can be gleaned from the latter portion of chapter seven.

The Present Difficulties. The first reason why Paul advises you to stay single is due to "the present distress" (7:26). In this, Paul originally was referring to the distressing conditions that faced first-century Christians. These conditions included fierce hatred, bitterness, and widespread persecutions for their faith.

Paul, personally, had experienced intense persecution. He had been beaten, thrown into prison, flogged with the torturous cat-o'-nine-tails, and even stoned and left for dead. He underwent all this and more for only one reason: he was a disciple of Jesus Christ, dedicated to the task of building His Kingdom.

What About Us? In view of this inevitable persecution of believers, Paul thought it best that single Christians remain unmarried. However, think about it. His advice may be more relevant now than it was on the day he penned those words! Even today in many foreign countries Christians are called on to deny Jesus or lose their own lives and those of their families.

The Shortness of Time. A second reason why Paul recommends single Christian living is because of the shortness of time (7:29). Paul reminds us that "the form of this world is passing away" (7:31). The apostle lived with a consciousness that the Lord Jesus could return at any moment. Everything he said or did had that imminent return of Christ as its backdrop.

It's Later Than We Think! Current events, viewed in the light of biblical prophecies, would lead us to believe that Paul's words are even more appropriate for this generation than they were for first-century believers. Consequently, "last-days Christians" need to be even more careful about getting too attached to the world. If we truly are the final generation of believers, it is imperative that we take seriously the radical demands upon our lives that Jesus Christ makes. Anything that is not going to last forever should be low on our priority lists.

Believe it or not, the marriage of a man and a woman is one of those things that will not last forever. Marriage is a magnificent part of this world, but will not be a part of eternity. It is not the sugar-sweet image that you often have of matrimony, but that is what Jesus said in Mark 12:25. In heaven, Jesus will be the husband, and the Church, all true believers, will be His wife. Apparently, marriage, as you know it now, will be superseded by membership in the heavenly Family of God.

Undivided Discipleship. Yet, Paul would have you be free from such divisive concerns (7:32) and that is precisely his third argument for the single Christian life. The apostle writes: ". . . One who is unmarried is concerned about the things of the Lord, how he may please the Lord; but one who is married is concerned about the things of the world, how he may please his wife, and his interests are divided. And the woman who is unmarried, and the virgin, is concerned about the things of the Lord, that she may be holy both in body and spirit; but one who is married is concerned about the things of the world, how she may please her husband" (7:32–34).

Paul is, once again, being a hard realist. He points out the oft-unspoken truth that it is easier for a single person to devote his full attention to the things of the Lord than it is for a married individual. Paul is not speaking negatively about marriage here. He is simply addressing the fact that marriage has responsibilities that can easily conflict with undistracted devotion and service to Jesus.

My Own Experience. The Watchmen ministry has kept me hustling for the past fifteen years. On many occasions, last-minute business trips have called me away from home. Concerts and speaking engagements have taken me to distant towns, states, and foreign countries, often with very little advance planning. Even at home, my schedule has been erratic.

Am I complaining? Not on your life! I would not have traded the past years of single ministry for all the money in the world! I have been able to do things for God, go places for God, taking advantage of available ministry opportunities that my fellow married ministers and colleagues have not.

Why? Not because I am any more "spiritual" than my married brothers and sisters; I am certainly no more talented or gifted. Basically, I have been able to do what I have done these past years because I have been single and, therefore, less encumbered than my brethren.

How Can You Best Glorify Jesus? This, of course, is the overriding factor in Paul's entire discussion of marriage versus singleness. So many times you get caught up in the search for what is going to make you happy, you neglect to deal with the issue of: "How can my life be most effective for God? How can my life count the most for Jesus?" This is the primary issue for every true disciple of Christ.

In my own life, the Lord had to break me free from my assumption of marriage. I had grown up presupposing that I would one day be married. Oh, yes, in the back of my mind, there was a suspicion that I might remain single. Still, I presumed that, in all probability, I would marry.

It was a major turning point in my social life and my spiritual life, when, on my knees before God, I came to the point where I could honestly pray, "Okay, Lord. If You want me to remain single, I'm willing to do that, just so long as You can use me for Your glory. You call the shots, Lord. If You want me married, I'm open to the idea, but You are going to have to bring the right girl into my life."

That may sound to you like a simple prayer, but to me, the ramifications were profound. Suddenly, I was out of the mate race. I had committed my life to Another.

No, I didn't quit dating altogether. In fact, I probably dated a greater variety of girls than ever! I was free to do so, because now I was not looking for a wife. Once I had it firmly embedded in my mind that I was going to let the Lord show me—not me trying to convince Him—who was right for me (if anyone), I was liberated to date young ladies just for the sake of enjoying a good time together.

Only within the past few years did I begin to sense that God was leading me out of singleness and into marriage. It was a slow, gradual process. He did not lead me to abruptly break with my single life-style and plunge headlong into marriage. By the time I got married, the Lord had gently weaned me away from singleness to make me thoroughly and unreservedly ready for marriage.

One word of caution: Be absolutely honest with your dates. If you have been given the gift of singleness so your life may count more for God, it would be deceitful of you to date the same person regularly without informing them of your commitment. If two Christians understand that they are dating "just for the fun of it" with no inclinations toward a future relationship, that is fine. However, if you are committed to a single life, and you date the same person more than a few times, you can't blame that person for getting the impression that you are seeking a more permanent setup. If you are not, tell your date so at the earliest juncture in your relationship, without forcing the issue. You may lose a date, but better to lose a date than to lose a brother or sister in the Lord!

Be sure to use a good measure of discretion and spiritual sensitivity when dealing with this situation, but be realistic as well. There is no need to preface every social encounter with the rapid-fire introduction, "Hi! My name is Willie Witness, and I don't ever plan to get married because God has given me the gift of singleness, but if you're not busy this Friday, would you like to go to the ball game with me?"

13

Help! I Want to Be Married!

Now comes one of the most crucial discussions of this book. That is: What should you do if you are single, and you want to be married, but the right person hasn't come along yet? How will you know that person? What qualities should you look for in your future marriage partner? Should you look for that person at all?

First of all, you need to understand that it is not wrong to want to be married. In fact, such desires are very right! Marriage is, as the familiar vows proclaim, an honorable estate. The Bible says, "Let marriage be held in honor among all . . ." (Hebrews 13:4).

It is almost fashionable nowadays to speak in a derogatory manner concerning marriage, but don't be misled. Demeaning attitudes toward marriage are not of God (1 Timothy 4:1–3).

Marriage is God's norm for most of His children. That does not mean that God regards married couples as normal, and single persons as abnormal. It does mean that most of you will get married, because that is God's "ordinary" way of working out His will in your lives. That is the way He usually does things. God does not promise a marriage partner for all of you, but the number of Christians called to a lifetime of singleness is extremely small when compared to the vast majority who are called to married life.

Some single Christians have confessed to me that they have believed that desiring to be married is sinful, or "less than spiritual," or untrusting of God's will for them. I am not suggesting that you develop a marriage obsession. Understand, though, it is not wrong to want marriage, to plan for marriage, and even to pray for your future marriage. But surely, it would be improper and potentially harmful and sinful to become frustrated over, preoccupied with, or overanxious about, finding your life partner.

While waiting for your mate, there are two points at which you should keep constant watch: (1) Be certain that you are walking daily in the center of God's will; (2) Be certain that you are trusting God to bring the right person into your life at the right time.

Let's Get Practical—A Checklist for the Altar-bound

Having established some of the more theological aspects of making certain that you are living according to God's will for your life, let's move on to the more practical areas of finding the mate that fits into God's plan for you. How can you be certain that Mr. or Miss Wonderful is the best possible marriage partner for you? Turning the question around, how will you be sure that you are the perfect mate for Mr. or Miss Right? What kind of person should you be, and what kind of person should you seek?

As with all relationships, there are only two foolproof tests: *time* and *prayer*. Still, consider a few basics.

Spiritual Qualities First. As a Christian contemplating married life, your primary goal should be to glorify Christ through your marriage. Therefore, you should be looking for a mate who is spiritually mature. If the person you are thinking about marrying doesn't measure up spiritually, you'd better think again, no matter how many good points that person has.

Establish in your heart and mind that you will not compromise your spiritual standards in any way. Only then are you ready to check out other compatibility factors concerning a mate.

Here's That Commonsense Checklist. I have discovered that people in love often cast all logic to the wind when it comes to romantic emotions versus commonsense evaluations. To help prevent this from happening to you, let me ask some hard questions.

For starters, do you and your potential mate genuinely like each other? "Like each other? Man, Ken! You're way behind on this thing! We don't just like each other; we *love* each other!"

Yeah; yeah; I hear you; but do you like to talk to each other? Do you enjoy simply being together? Can you laugh at each other without somebody getting offended? Can you argue with each other and then work out a meaningful solution, compromise, or reconciliation? Are you intimate friends, or are there subjects that you don't feel free to talk about with your possible mate?

Are you spiritually compatible? "What do you mean 'spiritually compatible'? We're both Christians. Isn't that enough?"

Nope. Can you pray together?

"Well ... you know, when our singles group prays. ..."

That's all fine, but I want to know if you can really spend time in prayer together. Can you see yourselves unashamedly on your knees pouring out your hearts before God, without fear, embarrassment, or hesitation? It may surprise you, but there are many Christian couples who find it difficult to pray together. Though you may develop this after marriage, honestly ask yourself how good your prayer life as a couple is now.

A further word concerning spiritual compatibility, particularly for you ladies: In considering a possible partner, be sure that he is at least as spiritually mature as you are, or shows potential of becoming so in the very near future. Otherwise, you are letting yourself in for trouble.

This guy is going to be the head of your household. He is going to be the spiritual leader of your family. He'd better have his relationship with the Lord pretty well together before you two tie the knot.

If you are a relatively mature Christian, you need a man of God to whom you can look for spiritual guidance, wisdom, fellowship, and perhaps, even instruction. You need a *man of God,* not a *babe in Christ!*

Do you share your partner's theological persuasions? "What? There he goes again with all that 'theological' stuff! I thought we were getting practical here."

This *is* practical. In fact, for two Christians, it may be imperative that you discuss your partner's theological positions prior to marriage. I know we like to rave about how God is not concerned about our denominations or our theologies, but even in this day of great spiritual unity, drastic differences in doctrine still divide disciples of Jesus.

"Yes, but as long as we're both Christians. . . ."

That's a good starting point, but there are many brands of Christianity. When it comes to marriage, save yourself some grief. Try to find yourself a mate who basically shares your beliefs concerning Christian practice and doctrine. Unless, of course, you'd prefer to spend your entire married life arguing theology! Certainly, two conflicting opinions can serve to sharpen one's intellectual and spiritual wits, but irreconcilable differences concerning the Christian life can also drive a wedge between the most godly of couples.

Avoid this mess. Seek a companion with whom you can spiritually relate and grow. You don't have to agree on every issue, but your marriage will flow much more smoothly if you agree more often than you disagree. Save the theological debates for the boardroom, not the bedroom.

How compatible are you and your partner in the area of education? Are you both relatively close in your intelligence levels? The "brain" and the "dingdong" make for nice romantic comedy, but the combination doesn't fare so well in real-life marriages. Does either one or both of you plan to further your education? If so, are you both prepared to make the sacrifices necessary to do so? Keeping a marriage together while going to school is not an impossible task, but it is a formidable one.

What about your professional goals? Where do you want to be in life ten years from now? Are you both satisfied with your jobs? Are there vocational sacrifices that you would be unwilling to make for the sake of your marriage? How does each of you feel about the working wife, the working mother? This is a particularly delicate dilemma for a woman who has her career in mind.

What are your attitudes about children? Do you want children? If so, when and how many? How do you feel about birth control? Many devout Christians have radically different views on the subject. What is yours? What is your partner's? Have you formed any ideas about child rearing and child discipline?

What are your attitudes about money? Have you and your partner talked about your attitudes concerning finances? Few newlyweds begin their marriages with a surplus of money. Consequently, for many couples, how they use what financial resources they have often becomes a sensitive sore spot. You do realize, don't you, that in marriage, money is not a yours-mine commodity; it is to be regarded as "ours." A good sign that you are nearing readiness for marriage is when you can willfully and cheerfully put your money where your mouth is!

Who is going to handle the checkbook? You? Your partner? Both of you? How many bank accounts will you need? How are you going to pay the monthly bills? More couples than you can imagine argue over who spent what, and why.

Do you have the same attitude about tithing? For the Christian couple, giving to God's work is not an option. The first 10 percent (tithe) of everything you have belongs to Him. After giving beyond the tithe, you begin to present God your offerings. How *does* your mate feel about tithing your income? your time? your talents? the giving of offerings?

What do you both regard as fiscal priorities? Are there things you would like to buy if you had the extra money? It would be wise to get a general idea of these things in advance of your marriage. That way, when your wife brings home a mink coat, or your husband pulls up in a fancy new sports car, it won't come as a total surprise to you!

What about a budget? How much money will it take to keep the two of you happy? Are you able to plan your spending policies and then stick to them? Are you willing to sacrifice your own personal luxuries for the sake of your household budget? Have you discussed exactly what married life is going to cost you both in dollars and cents?

How about saving money? I realize that thrift is an almost forgotten practice nowadays, but if you have never disciplined yourself to save money, you are not ready for marriage. Likewise, if you are considering marriage to a person who has never had a savings account, you'd better hold off a while, or else plan to spend a lot of time counting nickels and dimes, trying to make ends meet.

One other financial area that needs to be discussed with your partner is the matter of credit and the use of revolving charge accounts. Talking about fiscal responsibility is not most couples' idea of romantic conversation. Nevertheless, I cannot overestimate the importance of considering these questions prior to your wedding day. Many now-divorced couples did not.

Are your family backgrounds compatible? Another factor that may provide insight to the marriage potential of your partner is the area of family background and family relationships. "Romeo and Juliet" and "Cinderella" are wonderful stories of love triumphing over family background, but for most people, *socioeconomic similarities make for more secure marriages.*

If you are planning to marry someone who comes from a close family, *be prepared to make your future spouse's family your own.* The old saying "You don't marry a person, you marry a family" is true. One word of caution here: while filial ties are commendable, beware of the potential mate who is excessively reluctant to break those bonds in order to tie the knot with you. There is no room for Mama's apron strings in a good marriage.

Do you share similar leisure-time activities? Is your marriage candidate a sports nut, television addict, amusement-park freak, constant reader, music lover, or a photography fanatic? If so, you'd better at least acquire a tolerance for such activities, or else acquire a new potential marriage partner.

Are you the right age to marry? It is no secret that teenage marriages have minimal chances of survival. Marriage is for adults only. It is not for the person who is still unsettled in his ways, or unaccustomed to handling life-sized responsibilities. It is not for the selfish, the foolish, or the immature.

Age can be a deceptive standard. It is *maturity level* that counts. Still, most counselors recommend age twenty-four or twenty-five as being the best age for men to marry. Prime marriage age for women seems to be twenty-two or twenty-three years of age. These ages are merely guides, but statistics support the idea that a couple who foregoes matrimony until their midtwenties, has a much greater chance of their marriage staying together. Almost all counselors frown upon teenage marriages and marriages in which one partner is more than ten to fifteen years older than the other.

Get a Second Opinion. It may sound odd, but seek out an unbiased advisor. Many couples, headstrong in love, ignore the vast pool of wisdom resources available to them. The Bible, however, advises us to seek wise spiritual counselors (*see* Proverbs 24:6; 19:20; 15:22; 12:15).

Nowadays, competent Christian counselors are readily available. If there are not two or three on your block or in your church, you need not despair. You can still take advantage of books, tapes, seminars, films, and filmstrips on nearly every aspect of love, sex, dating, marriage, singleness, and even divorce. Many of these are exceptionally fine sources of wisdom, and would be of value to all

Christians. They should be considered as prerequisites by anyone who is seriously contemplating marriage.

One of the best sources of counsel, if you are considering marriage, is *your family.* Friends may be helpful, as well. The advice of friends, though, should be taken with the proverbial grain of salt. Friends often have a tendency to reinforce the same thoughts and attitudes you have. Otherwise, you probably wouldn't be friends. Your family may be a more reliable source of wisdom.

If your family members don't react somewhat positively toward your potential mate, you would be wise to reconsider. Your family knows you. They have put in a lot more time with you than your partner has. If they don't give the impression that they are happy about your relationship, there may be some valid reasons for their feelings. The odds are in your favor if you pay close attention to their counsel. Remember, they love you and care about your future.

God's Word Is God's Will. God will never contradict His Holy Word with guidance contrary to His already revealed will. That is why most counselors confidently assert that most of God's will for your life is already known. All you have to do is pick up your Bible and study it to find out what God wants for you. Notice, though, I said you must "study" the Bible. It will be utterly impossible for you to accurately discover God's will for your life without a working knowledge of God's Word. Furthermore, I can almost guarantee you that unless you become thoroughly familiar with the Lord's general plan for your life, you will miss His will in the specifics as well, particularly in the matter of a marriage partner.

14

Believing for the Best!

I was tearing down my drums following the Watchmen's presentation at "Creation," a weekend "Jesus festival" that annually attracts more than 25,000 people from all across the eastern United States. I was tired, but spiritually exhilarated from the evening's events. My packing chores were interrupted when, from out of the darkness beyond the well-lighted stage area, I heard a dignified female voice call, "Mr. Abraham. Mr. Abraham! May I talk with you, please?"

Unaccustomed to such formality (at a festival, everyone is "Brother" or "Sister"), I was intrigued. I descended from the drum platform and walked to the end of the stage. Squinting into the blackness, I scanned the crowd of bystanders in search of a serious face to match the earnest voice that had called my name.

"Pardon me. Here I am!"

I whirled around and found myself facing a well-dressed woman, approximately thirty-five years of age.

"Oh, hi! What can I do for you?"

"Mr. Abraham," she proceeded in a businesslike manner. "I heard you say from the stage tonight Jesus loves us, and if we trust Him, He will provide exactly what we need. Well, I need a marriage partner; can I trust God for that?"

131

I gulped hard before stating firmly: "Yes, I believe you can."
And I do!

Trusting God with your desire for a marriage partner, however, is no easy task. To really trust Him with your social life means: (1) you believe God wants the best for you; (2) you are confident He will bring the proper person into your life in His perfect time (which will be ideal time for you, as well).

But Beware of Satan's Tricks

Be aware, the devil may try to sidetrack you. He will dangle doubts before you. Satan may say, "Sure, you believe that God knows the right person for you to marry. But what are you going to do if you never find that person? What then? Think of all that you've wasted while you've been waiting! You could have been having a good time all these years, but you've blown it! It's too late for you now. Why wait any longer? You're getting older every day, and you're letting life slip right through your fingertips!"

Sometimes, Satan tries to sneak a spiritual-sounding slider in on you. "You had the right one, but you messed up! You had the opportunity to have God's choice for you, but you let that person go. You have missed out on God's best for you! Now, you are doomed to settle for second-best."

Who Is the "Who" That Brings Together?

I love the passage in the Bible that says: " . . . What therefore God has joined together, let no man separate" (Matthew 19:6). Notice that it is "God" who does the joining together of two lives, not a computer dating service, or some self-ordained ecclesiastical cupid.

How liberating a concept it was when I finally realized God wanted to provide the perfect partner for me! Prior to this, I was constantly jostling to place myself in the "right position" to receive

God's person for me. I would attend Christian gatherings with the notion that at any moment, God was going to drop a gorgeous, godly girl onto the ground in front of me, with a sign hung across her chest: SPECIAL DELIVERY FOR MR. KENNETH ABRAHAM!

Many times, I would see an attractive young woman and endeavor to maneuver myself into a position where meeting her was practically inevitable. I was not distrusting God; I was merely trying to help Him out a little! Oftentimes, I would make the young lady's acquaintance and strike up a dating relationship with her, only to find out later that it wasn't worth the time or effort. I'm sure she would say the same.

Gradually, I came to the point where I would not even date someone on a casual basis unless I could detect a good measure of future marriage potential in the relationship. This seemed more "spiritual" to me, and in a sense, it was, since spiritual characteristics were at the top of my list of marriage prerequisites. Nevertheless, I was being just as silly; I was *still* trying to handle my own social life, although being more selective in my search for Miss Perfect.

I began to wonder, "Where am I ever going to find her?" I surmised that God's woman for me would most likely be found in Christian circles. Consequently, I began to attend every Bible-study group, Christian fellowship activity, or church service I could fit into my schedule. I'd walk in, look around, and say, "Okay, Lord. Where is she?"

Certainly, you need to be in fellowship with Christians of the opposite sex if you are going to discover your marriage partner. If you are seeking a mate, it only makes sense to go where the boys are, or where the girls are. Some Christian counselors take offense at this advice. They say that to consciously place yourself in an environment where there are more available potential partners is to invite self-will rather than trust in God. I disagree.

Be careful of your motives, though. If your main purpose in attending a particular Christian function is to find a mate, you are wasting your time. You are going to miss God's blessing, some tremendous spiritual experiences, and probably your mate, as well!

"Okay, if I'm going to trust God to bring Mr. Right into my life, what about my list of characteristics?" an intelligent businesswoman asked me. "Should I decide what kind of person I'm looking for, or should I just passively trust God to bring what's best for me?"

"Both," I answered her.

What about those lists? I had mine. (Doesn't every single person have a list of his or her future marriage partner's qualifications?) Knowing what qualities you are looking for in a mate is an invaluable aid in choosing your marriage partner. Nevertheless, you need to be open to what God wants for you. Otherwise, there is a tendency to become overly dependent upon your list. This can work against you in two ways. First, by holding too tightly to your preconceived notions of what you want, you may inadvertently lock yourself in on a person who may not be God's best for you. Second, by rigidly limiting the possibilities to what you think you need, you may miss some splendid opportunities for spiritual growth and fellowship with members of the opposite sex who do not fit the descriptions on your list, but who may be exactly what God has in mind for you.

If your list is to be of any value to you, you need to keep it flexible. Be sure to allow a lot of blank spaces where God can fill in the details. Otherwise, if you stick to what you think you want, measuring by your own limited vision and resources, you are liable to set your sights much too low. (God always has something much better in store for us than we do for ourselves!)

Is There a "One and Only"?

A wide-eyed freshman asked, "Does that mean there is only one person in all the world that God has for me, and if I miss that one person, I am doomed to a subquality marriage, even though I want God's best in my life?"

Questions of this nature, though sincere, are frequently irrelevant. If you truly are walking in God's path for your life, and trusting Him totally, He will bring that special person into your life (assuming you are to be married), and you will run very little risk in identifying your partner. It is only when your life with Christ is inconsistent that the issues become clouded.

Hit or Miss. In the early stages of the USA space program, NASA was able to have two separate spacecraft meet and interlock millions of miles above the earth. Both crafts were guided by accurate scientific principles and kept on course by constant corrective measures administered by "Mission Control." There were millions of obstacles in outer space that either of the ships could have encountered prior to their linkage. Had either craft collided with a foreign object, the results would have been disastrous. The yoking and subsequent mission were successful, though, for three reasons:

1. The two spacecraft were designed for each other;

2. They each stayed in immediate and intimate contact with their source until their separate trajectories met and interlocked;

3. They continued to follow directions and guidance administered by their source after they united.

The same factors are relevant when we speak of God bringing two marriage partners together. If the adherence to scientific principles and human wisdom can reap such astounding results in outer space, cannot our God do something similar in our "inner space"? Is it too difficult to believe that our all-wise God is able to design and bring together two of His obedient children who will be the ideal marriage partners for each other? Where is our faith? Dare we trust Him for less?

Uniquely Yours. Won't it be wonderful on your wedding day to look at the person to whom you are about to commit your life and know that he or she is God's will for your life? Good. Acceptable. Perfect for you! Such an ideal is not mere marital mush; it is God's norm for every Christian marriage. Only a fool would marry with less certainty.

If You're Not Sure, Wait! If you are contemplating marriage, I believe that God will give you definite, indisputable direction that you and your partner are right for each other. If you do not have that peace, you would be wise to forego your wedding until you do. If, after a reasonable amount of time and prayer, such a calm does not come, your safest action would be to abandon immediate hopes of marriage to that person.

Sadly, many couples plunge headlong into matrimony without conclusive evidence that God wants them together. Such marriages usually travel stormy seas, and are, oftentimes, shattered on relatively small rocks or reefs.

Getting Back to the Question. This brings us full-circle to the wide-eyed freshman's question, "If I miss God's best, does that mean that I am doomed to a subquality marriage?"

I have wrestled with the ramifications of my answer for years. As such, it is not without a great deal of previous thought and consideration that I must sadly answer, "Yes, if you miss God's best for your life, you are forced to accept a less fulfilling marriage than what God originally intended for you."

Before you slam this book shut in anger and despair, let me explain why I have come to this conclusion. *Understand!* There is no *need* to miss God's choice for you. After all, He has supplied many sources of wisdom from which you may draw in making this important decision. He has given you His written, authoritative Word, the Bible, for your guidance. He has endowed you with common sense. He has raised up wise spiritual counselors, whose opinions and insights He expects you to use. If necessary, in some cases, God will even provide supernatural signs to lead His children in the proper direction.

If you choose to ignore this stack of resources, you will have no excuse for choosing the wrong mate, and missing God's best for your life. You will have nobody to blame but yourself.

What Went Wrong? The grim realities of life pinch at our spiritual idealism. Unfortunately, there are some marriages that were ordained by God, begun in the Spirit, and ended in divorce. What happened? Somebody didn't keep it together. Maybe both partners failed to keep it together. They didn't cultivate their relationship with the Lord and, consequently, their relationship with each other fell prey to the same pressures that plague a non-Christian marriage. Maybe it was selfishness, lust, greed, pride, jealousy. Whatever it was, it wasn't from God!

Herein lies a word of warning, yet also a ray of hope. If you miss God's choice for your life, *He demands that you remain with your original selection.* Fortunately, God has a marvelous way of cleaning up your messes! When you sin, whether by choice or mistake, He can still salvage your life if you will repent and then allow Him to run the remainder of your life. If, even after an unwise choice or a willful transgression of His revealed will, you humbly seek His help, He will forgive; He will cleanse, He will heal and restore.

15

Prepare to Meet Thy Mate!

While you are waiting for God to bring Mr. or Miss Perfect into your life, you will want to avoid those creepy, crawling creatures that seem bent on destroying your fruitfulness. Aside from playing defense, warding off worms, what positive action should a single Christian take?

Two practices are paramount: *prepare* and *pray*. Let's look at them individually.

Start preparing to be a maximum marriage partner right now! Everything you will be in your future marriage relationship, you are developing today. Your basic personality and character traits will not magically change for the better the week before your wedding, so use your single days to prepare physically, mentally, emotionally, and spiritually. Make every *single* day count! Develop your career. Develop the gifts and ministries God has given to you. Don't just mope around the house, mulling over your lack of a mate. Get moving! Get busy for God, for your country, for your family, for yourself!

Of course, one's greatest aspiration, whether single or married, should be to become a man or woman of God. But what is a man of God? What should a woman of God be? Let's start with the women.

What a Woman!

Perhaps the classic description of a godly mate is found in Proverbs 31. Here, we find more than twenty-four characteristics of an excellent wife. Most of these qualities are equally applicable to a single woman, since nearly all of them could have been cultivated during this lady's single years.

The kind of woman described in Proverbs 31 is difficult to find. The writer of the passage admits, "An excellent wife, who can find? For her worth is far above jewels" (vs. 10). This lady is so highly touted in Scripture, many modern-day men and women view her as a biblical Bionic Bombshell! Many women have written her off as a lofty ideal, a woman to admire, but certainly not a practically attainable role model. Many men have decided that although this lady is more valuable than jewels, rare gems are easier to find than Wonder Woman.

Nevertheless, the proverb is included in Scripture for a reason. "This passage is designed to show women what kind of wives they should be and to show men what kind of women they should choose to marry," says Linda Dillow in *Creative Counterpart*. Keep that in mind as we look at her.

The woman in Proverbs 31 is one who . . .

- *can be trusted* (v. 11).
- *does her husband good* (v. 12).
- *is a worker* (v. 13).
- *is an adventurous shopper* (v. 14).
- *is an early riser* (v. 15).
- *is a wise investor* (v. 16).
- *is a strong woman* (v. 17).
- *is self-confident* (v. 18).
- *is a night owl, too* (v. 18).
- *is a fashion designer* (v. 19).

- *has a heart of compassion* (v. 20).
- *has the pride of her man* (v. 23).
- *is an entrepreneur* (v. 24).
- *has a positive attitude* (v. 25).
- *speaks wisdom* (v. 26).
- *has a family which appreciates her* (v. 29).

Right Priorities. After pointing out this woman's attributes, the proverb closes with a revelation of our lady's formula for successful femininity. Surprisingly, it is not a bunch of dos and don'ts, but an attitude of heart. "Charm is deceitful and beauty is vain, but a woman who fears the Lord, she shall be praised" (v. 30).

A woman who fears the Lord will have a radiant beauty about her even in the absence of artificial adornments. This woman has a respect for the person of God, the Word of God, and the things of God. As such, she has a healthy self-respect. She takes care of and develops the body and mind God has given her, knowing that inward beauty only gets better with age.

Girls! Don't be duped by what you see on TV or read in the fashion magazines! The plastic, painted-up, slick-chick may be some guys' fantasy of a one-night affair, but few guys want to marry her. When a man starts thinking in terms of marriage, whether he is conscious of it or not, his mind turns to qualities that sound a lot like the woman in Proverbs 31. Men still look for women who are trustworthy, loyal, committed, hardworking, and good home managers. Most guys want their wives to be wise investors, generously giving, strong yet compassionate, cautious in speech yet quick to speak a word of kindness. Yes, ladies; believe it or not, most men still look for that kind of woman! If she has physical beauty to go along with these other traits, that is an added plus. Without these qualities, external and transient attractiveness will quickly fade, and a smart guy knows it!

The woman pictured in Proverbs 31 is truly a complete person. She is an individual who makes good use of her talents and abilities, while remaining sensitive and loving to all those around her. She is not a subservient slave. Neither is she a lazy, demanding witch. This woman has earned her right to be respected through her actions and attitudes. She has learned well the tenuous art of balancing her outside interests with those of her home. She is, at the same time, an industrious, ambitious businesswoman and an outstanding choice for "Mother and Wife of the Year."

Just as First Corinthians 13 is a true picture of what love is to be, Proverbs 31 is the image of what a woman of God is to be. It is an attainable goal toward which every Christian woman should aspire.

Well, how did you do, girls? Are you a woman of God? How do you measure up against the woman of Proverbs 31? Does she sound a lot like you? Better still, do you sound a lot like her? (Several in-depth discussions of Proverbs 31 are available, including Jill Briscoe's *Queen of Hearts* and Linda Dillow's *Creative Counterpart*.)

Front and Center, Fellows

Okay, girls; take a break. Sit back and relax while we investigate what it means to be a real man of God. Again, guys, this is the sort of man you should aim to be; girls, this is the kind of man you should have in mind when you start thinking of marriage.

There is no one passage of Scripture for men that serves as Proverbs 31 does for women. God's instructions to His men are sprinkled all over the Bible. There are, however, two passages that make for a clear composite picture of the man of God. These passages are 1 Timothy 3:1–7 and Titus 1:5–10. Paul is the author of both passages and in each, he is writing to one of his fellow workers. The apostle's instructions were specifically intended for the one who wished to become an overseer in the early church. An overseer was an elder, or bishop, a leader in the local congregation. Clearly, though, Paul considers these standards to be the norm for every Christian man.

The apostle lists at least twenty characteristics of a godly man.

These are qualities of the man with whom God is pleased. These traits have little to do with a fellow's office in life or his marital status. Paul is simply describing what it means to be God's man, married or otherwise.

Note, too, as we look at this list, that these are not spiritual gifts; most of these are personality traits that must be developed through discipline and dedication. Nineteen of the twenty qualifications "have to do with a man's reputation, ethics, morality, temperament, habits, and spiritual and psychological maturity. And the other one has to do with his ability to lead his own family," writes Gene A. Getz in *The Measure of a Man.*

He's Aboveboard. Paul begins his list with a summary. He says to Timothy that a man of God "must be above reproach." In other words, he should have a *good reputation.* This is a general overview of the man Paul intends to describe. A fellow's character should be highly regarded by the Christian community, at large, and especially by those in positions of spiritual leadership.

Proper View of Marriage. Paul also says that God's man is "the husband of one wife" (1 Timothy 3:2). This does not mean that a guy has to be married in order for him to be spiritually mature. It does mean that a Christian man should have a high and holy view of marriage. If he is married, he is committed to his wife for life. He does not bounce from one divorce to another. The man of God has a biblical understanding of what marriage is all about. Even if he is single, God's man will always regard the marriage relationship as sacred and something to be protected and maintained at all costs. Except in unusual cases, divorce is not an option for God's man. Any guy who looks at marriage through the escape hatch of divorce has a long way to go in becoming a man of God.

He's an Unshakable Character. A man of God is also "temperate" (1 Timothy 3:2). The word *temperate* usually conjures up pictures of a guy who doesn't eat too much, drink too much, or do anything else too much. He is moderate in all of his behavior. Paul, however, expands the meaning of the word. To the apostle, *temperate* connotes a man who is a stable fellow. He is a steadfast and

clear thinker. He doesn't get shook easily. The same word is sometimes translated as "sober" (1 Thessalonians 5:6), meaning a guy
who is able to stay cool, to keep his wits about him, not one who
quickly loses his orientation.

This sort of fellow is fairly self-confident, though not egotistical
or self-righteous. He has a positive outlook. He is self-disciplined
and knows how to exercise self-control. These qualities govern his
actions concerning food, drink, sex, even the way he uses his leisure
time.

Solid As a Rock. The man of God is "prudent" (1 Timothy 3:2).
The word *prudent* is closely akin to *temperate in* that it also evokes
images of a sober, sensible person. Still another meaning of *prudent*
has to do with inward self-control. Thus, the prudent man will be
morally chaste, having control over his mind and spirit, as well as
his body.

A Good Citizen. The man of God is also "respectable" (1 Timothy
3:2). The word implies a man who is well-behaved, orderly, honorable in all his conduct. He is a good, moral citizen who lives his life
according to biblical principles.

He'll Give Himself Away. The Christian man must also be "hospitable" (1 Timothy 3:2; Titus 1:8). In ancient cultures, including
Jewish society, showing hospitality to strangers was not an option.
It was the only acceptable practice. This carried over to Christianity. As such, a man of God was expected to use his home as a means
of reaching out to the nonbelievers in his community. His home was
also to be a haven for fellow Christians.

Sadly, many modern Christians have ignored their responsibilities to be hospitable, while cults, pimps, and pushers have made
multitudes of converts by offering a helping hand and an open door.
We gladly give financial gifts to our favorite charities, but we cringe
at the thought of having a tramp into our homes for dinner and an
evening of company. We send money to missionaries in Malaysia,
but we won't invite the neighborhood kids in for Bible study. We'll
pay to put the evangelist up in a swanky hotel, just as long as we
don't have to open our home to him.

All the while, we have numerous biblical injunctions to give of ourselves to help meet the needs of others. Paul encourages the Romans to "practice hospitality" (Romans 12:13). Peter wrote, "Be hospitable to one another without complaint" (1 Peter 4:9). The writer to the Hebrews encouraged his readers with the intriguing thought, "Do not neglect to show hospitality to strangers, for by this some have entertained angels without knowing it" (Hebrews 13:2). Mmm ... I wonder if I've entertained any angels lately!

A Good Example. God's man must also be "able to teach" (1 Timothy 3:2; Titus 1:9). This is not the "gift of teaching" mentioned elsewhere in Paul's letters; it is a characteristic and attitude of one's personality. It has often been rightly said, "Christianity is better caught than taught." The man of God must teach with his life. Everything about him should show Christ to the world.

Obviously, in order to teach others about Jesus, a man of God must know Him intimately and have a working knowledge of His Word. He must also develop practical ways of relating to other people. It will do him no good to be armed with the "sword of the Spirit," if he uses that sword to cut other people to shreds. Being able to teach, then, implies personal maturity and an ability to communicate spiritual truths through example, as well as word.

He's Not a Boozer. A Christian man should be one who is "not addicted to wine" (1 Timothy 3:3; Titus 1:7). A few years ago, we could casually mention this and keep going. Nowadays, many Christians have so confused liberty with license, that the matter of overindulgence merits our close attention.

Here, as in other areas of a Christian's convictions, two factors must be considered. First, what will drinking do to your Christian testimony? Like it or not, in our culture, the secular world has an image that Christians do not imbibe. When you are seen (or even known to be) drinking, your testimony is almost always compromised.

Second, while you may be able to have a drink, walk away, and be relatively unmarred, a person who is struggling with his desire to overdrink may say, "Well, if he can do it, so can I." One drink for him, though, may lead to another, another, then to impairment of his mental and motor faculties, and, ultimately, to drunkenness and sin. By your poor example, you have caused a weaker person to stumble and sin.

Furthermore, staggering statistics on teenage alcoholism, alcohol-related auto accidents, divorce, child abuse, and other forms of immorality connected to drinking are evidence enough to keep me from drinking. The question "Should a Christian drink?" seems superfluous in the light of alcohol's blight upon our society.

"Yeah, but getting drunk is no worse than overeating," someone calls out from the back of the room.

"No, it's not," I answer. "No worse, but no better either. Both are sin. To me, a grossly overweight Christian is as displeasing to God as is the drunk on the street corner. Both are mistreating their bodies. It's pretty tough to talk to a drug addict, or a boozer, or a smoker about deliverance and self-control while your stomach is blocking the view of your toes!

"There is one big difference, though. I haven't met too many innocent people who have been victimized by someone else's overeating problem. I have met a lot of people whose lives have been tragically scarred by somebody who drank too much."

A man of God should not be addicted to wine, and women, you should keep that in mind when you are considering a marriage partner. Booze and marriage don't mix.

Easy Does It. In his letter to Titus, Paul places the term "quick-tempered" right next to addicted to wine and being pugnacious (1:7). Clearly, a man who leans toward drunkenness and brawling is often a fellow who flies off the handle pretty easily, too.

Most quick-tempered people are spoiled brats, selfish, or insecure. In any case, they make lousy marriage partners.

A Gentleman. Contrary to being belligerent, always looking for a fight or an argument, the man of God is to be "gentle" (*see* 1 Timothy 3:2,3; Titus 3:2). Paul is not suggesting that Christian men be weak or effeminate. He is talking about a gentleness that is couched in strength, especially strength of character. This is strength with control. The title to Joyce Landorf's marvelous book sums up the balanced male equation: *Tough and Tender.*

Paul recommends this trait, and he doesn't strike me as a twerpy sort of guy. Anyone who could take the physical abuse he did, without giving up, is not my idea of a sissy.

Jesus was not exactly a gutless guru, either. He displayed tremendous intestinal fortitude, yet He was also gentle. In describing Himself, He once said, "Take My yoke upon you, and learn from Me, for I am gentle and humble in heart; and you shall find rest for your souls" (Matthew 11:29). Interesting, isn't it? The only place where Jesus describes His own personality, He uses two words that most modern-day men would be reluctant to have ascribed to their character: gentle and humble.

In a society that seems to glorify the violent, the crude, the rude, and the inconsiderate, many men view gentleness as a compromise of their masculinity. Some men don't know how to be gentle, or even that God says they should be. Sadly, this is often true of Christian men, as well as nonbelievers.

A man of God should seek to be gentle. A wise woman of God should seek a relationship only with a gentleman who is also a gentle man.

No Chip on This Shoulder. God's man is "uncontentious" (1 Timothy 3:3). This means that he is not quarrelsome. Let's look further at what a man of God is not. He is not one for fussin', fightin', and feudin'. He is not always looking to stir up trouble. He does not have to get his own way. He does not have to be the "big cheese." He is not an authoritarian leader; he is not a dictator in his family, business, or church relationships. He is not given to cursing, cutting sarcasm, or criticism. He *is* the exact opposite of those things.

Women: If your guy exhibits a general attitude of contentiousness, always going around with a chip on his shoulder, it is not a sign of masculinity. It is a sign of immaturity. You are foolish if you remain in that relationship.

Guys: If you notice that you have a tendency to be contentious, understand that God is not pleased with you. He wants you to mature spiritually, and part of that involves getting rid of your contentiousness. Ask Him to show you its cause. It may be jealousy, insecurity, selfishness, or some other violation of God's Word. The Lord will show you the source of your sin, if you will give Him the opportunity.

Not Greedy. The man of God must also be "free from the love of money" (1 Timothy 3:3). How vital it is for a Christian man to have a proper attitude toward money and the things it will purchase! This is especially important in marriage, but is equally true for a single guy.

Understand: there is nothing inherently evil about money. You are not necessarily more "spiritual" simply because you are broke. Money is basically neutral. It is neither right nor wrong, good nor bad. It is the *"love* of money" that is an offense to God.

Money, similar to any other gift of God, can become an idol, a curse. When we seek after the gift rather than the Giver, we will lose the One who gives to us. For many, money becomes their god. They live to make more dollars. They seek to lay up treasures in this world, forgetting Jesus' stern words, "Do not lay up for yourselves treasures upon earth. . . . But lay up for yourselves treasures in heaven, where neither moth nor rust destroys, and where thieves do not break in or steal; for where your treasure is, there will your heart be also" (Matthew 6:19–21). Obviously, a lot of people have been investing in the wrong bank!

It is no secret that at the heart of many marriage problems, many church conflicts, and many international disputes, there is a dollar bill. Perhaps, that is why Paul warned so adamantly that God's man should be free from the love of the stuff.

However, there is nothing wrong with Christians having money. It is when money has "us" that there are problems. Remember, "to whom much is given, much is required" (*see* Luke 12:48).

Ladies: if you are looking for a man of God, be especially scrutinizing of your man's attitude toward his wallet and his bankbook. He cannot love both Almighty God and the Almighty Dollar.

A Take-Charge Guy. We now come to a most telling test of a Christian man. "He must be one who manages his own household well . . ." (1 Timothy 3:4). Here, Paul is not just talking about handling household financial affairs, or keeping the lawn neat, or the roof repaired. He is referring to a man whose whole life is in accordance with God's principles of attitude and conduct. He's got his life together with the Lord, and all of his interpersonal relationships are pleasing to God. If our Christianity is real anywhere, it must be real at home. If a guy doesn't maintain his Christian life among his family members, it certainly won't work out in the world.

He Is Spiritually Mature. Paul writes that an overseer, or leader in the church, must not be a new convert (1 Timothy 3:6), no matter how glowing is his testimony, or how sincere and enthusiastic he may be. If a guy is going to lead in the Church of God, he needs time to grow and mature in his relationship with Christ. At this point, spiritual maturity is far more important than chronological age.

This same standard should be enforced when it comes to Christian marriage. A fellow who becomes a believer in Christ needs to develop spiritually, regardless of how old he is, before he can become the spiritual leader in a marriage. Most guys need a minimum of six months to a year to become established in their new Christian faith. The great apostle Paul spent the first three years of his new Christian life simply getting his own head together, settling in his own heart what he believed, and coming to grips with the Gospel's radical claims upon his life-style. Nowadays, a guy becomes a Christian, and you want to make him a Sunday-school teacher, a choir leader, and a youth worker—all in a matter of weeks!

It doesn't work that way. It takes time, study, and discipline to become a mature man of God.

Ladies: make it a rule! Never even *consider* marriage to a new believer! In fact, you need to be very cautious about dating a new believer. A babe in Christ needs to be nurtured with the same loving care that a newborn baby in the hospital requires. His spiritual health is of primary importance, at this point, not your big date for the Sunday-school picnic! Give him time to grow. I know there aren't a lot of Christian guys in your town, but if you interfere with the initial spiritual strengthening of this one, there is liable to be one less around.

Remember, give him six to twelve months to mature. A new Christian guy needs at least that much time to establish his own spiritual orientation. It is too much to ask of him to be responsible for the spiritual life of a wife just yet. He is still adjusting, becoming acclimated to a whole new world. He is experiencing different thought patterns, new desires, emotions, and setting new goals. The best thing you can do for him is to help him get firmly rooted in the Word of God.

Men: obviously, if you are a new believer in Jesus, you should not seek a wife for a while. You are not ready to be the spiritual leader to your future wife and children until you grow strong in your relationship with Jesus.

You may be a good businessman, a talented professional, or a highly educated intellectual, but you are not qualified to marry one of "God's Chosen Women" until you have established a deep and lasting relationship with Christ. If you are a new Christian guy, with hopes of marrying a Proverbs 31 sort of woman, get busy becoming a First Timothy type of man.

He Knows What's Happening. This man is "sensible" (Titus 1:8). He is not a wild-eyed fanatic. The man of God knows what he believes and why he believes it. His faith is not illogical or irrational; it is firmly founded upon the fact of God's Word. He does not park his brain outside the church before entering.

Because his judgments and decisions are grounded in the Word of God, the Christian man is "just" (Titus 1:8). A just man is a righteous man; not self-righteous, but truly a man who has learned how to live a practical, holy life. "Just" is not a catch-all term, but it is an all-encompassing, overall description of a Christian man.

Filled With the Holy Spirit. It follows, then, that this man is "devout" (Titus 1:8). Paul does not use the word *devout* as loosely as we do, today. He is talking about a man who is committed to a life of holiness, a life free from sin and wickedness. A devout man is devoted, of course; he is totally devoted to Christ, unreservedly His.

The opposite of a Spirit-filled life is a self-willed life. Selfishness is absolutely antithetical to God. It is disgusting in His sight and in the sight of our fellowman. It is possibly the root cause of most, if not all, sin. Self says, "I want what I want, and I am not going to let God's Word or anything else keep me from having my way." Self-centered people have "*I*-trouble."

Clearly, a mature man of God is one who has laid aside the old self and has "put on the new self, which in the likeness of God has been created in righteousness and holiness of the truth" (Ephesians 4:22–24). He is nothing less than Spirit-filled.

Well, guys, how do you fare? Are you a *man of God?* Or, at least, are you well on your way to becoming one? How do you stack up against Paul's instructions to Timothy and Titus? Are you growing more Christlike each day? Have you been filled with the Holy Spirit? Are you living daily under the Spirit's control? This is what it means to be a man of God.

Getting It All Together

"Wait a minute, Ken!" a young woman stopped me, as I taught on this subject. "If that is so, and I, as a woman of God, want to marry a man of God, does it follow that I should marry only a sanctified, Spirit-filled Christian guy?"

"Ideally, yes," I answered. "But remember, we are talking about spiritual maturity here, not a sinless perfection. Not all Christians are at the same maturity levels. We're not talking about a spiritual superman marrying a spiritual superwoman and then living out the perfect marriage happily ever after. There is no such thing as a perfect marriage. Nevertheless, in order to have a 'maximum marriage,' you need a man and a woman who are willing to surrender their lives completely to the One who is Perfect, and then be willing to work with and adjust to each other. Obviously, then, the marriage that has the best chance at success is the one in which a mature man of God is united with a mature woman of God."

If you are waiting upon God's choice of your marriage partner, don't just waste your time. Set yourself to the task of becoming the person God wants you to be. Prepare yourself! You won't remove all the risks involved. Marriage is always something of a risk, as is any human relationship. Nevertheless, by doing things God's way, you have every reason to be confident that your marriage will succeed. After all, as the saying goes, "God doesn't sponsor any flops!"

Granted, you may have to walk on by a few good-looking apples, shake you head, sigh, and say, "That's just not what I am looking for. There's a better one somewhere in the bunch. Lord, I will wait till You show me which one is best for me."

16

Pray, Baby! Pray!

I was standing alongside a seemingly sophisticated Christian counselor, when a young lady approached him with the question, "Doctor, I have done all that I know how to do in order to find God's mate for me. I am growing spiritually, and I am trying to improve in other areas, as well. What more can I do?"

I was surprised when the usually verbose counselor replied simply, "Pray, Baby! Pray!"

At first, I thought the highly regarded sage was being trite with her. I felt that the sincere question of the perplexed young woman deserved a more elaborate answer. Upon reflection, though, I realized that the man had given the only acceptable answer.

Prayer is the most important key to success. Prayers concerning your future marriage partner should include at least two elements: prayer for your mate and prayer for yourself.

God's Perfect Person

I have already emphasized the legitimacy of praying that God will bring your future spouse to you. Persistent prayers concerning marriage are not indicative of weak faith or a lack of trust. At different times, Jesus encouraged both a restful trust in His sovereign plan and the fervent beseeching of our heavenly Father. Certainly, during your single days, there will be occasions for both attitudes.

"Just claim her, Brother!" a simplistic saint used to suggest to me. "Just claim God's woman for you, then sit back and relax till she gets here!" I tried that and it didn't work!

Please don't misunderstand. I believe in claiming my requests whenever I know that I am praying *according to the will of God*. The Bible says: ". . . if we ask anything according to His will, He hears us. And if we know that He hears us in whatever we ask, we know that we have the requests which we have asked from Him" (1 John 5:14, 15). When I pray according to the will of God, in the name of Jesus, I can confidently assert that I "have" my request. How can I miss? Of course, the secret to success in this type of prayer is finding out what God's will in the matter really is!

Don't be afraid to ask God to bring you your mate, but while you are praying in this manner, be careful that you do not allow your desire for a spouse to overshadow your desire for the Lord. Remember, you must always seek Christ *first!*

Your Future Mate

Pray that God will provide your mate, but also, pray "for" your future husband or wife. By praying *for* your mate, I mean praying on his or her behalf. Pray about the hurts and needs that person is undergoing right now. Pray concerning the victories and the achievements your mate-to-be is experiencing.

"Wait, wait, wait a minute!" I hear you objecting. "How can I pray for this person I haven't even met yet?"

So you haven't met yet; so what? Does that mean you can't begin praying on behalf of your future partner? Obviously, your mate is living somewhere today, unless, of course, you are not planning to get married for the next twenty or thirty years, and then hope to hook someone nearly half your age! You didn't think God was going to start growing your spouse today, did you? No? Good! Then you are most likely going to marry someone who is currently battling with a lot of the same problems that you are. God is molding and refining that person just as He is doing something similar in your life. He is getting the two of you ready for each other.

Why not start praying for that other person right now? *Young man:* pray that God will develop in her the character she will need to be your wife. Pray for her emotional needs, for her sexual needs; not merely that she will be able to stand against temptation and remain pure, but also that she will begin to establish a healthy, biblical attitude toward sex. Pray for her social and intellectual needs to be met; that God will surround her with influences that will help her become all that she can be. Pray that her spiritual life will blossom and continue to grow, that she will fall ever more deeply in love with Jesus.

Young woman: you should begin praying today for the man of God who is to be your husband. Pray that God will develop in him the character traits that he will need to be the leader in your relationship, the God-ordained head of the household. Ask the Lord to teach him how to be a servant, for it is only in this manner that he will be able to love you, his wife, as Christ loved the Church (Ephesians 5:25).

Pray that he is able to complete his education and find a job in which he can derive a sense of satisfaction. Pray for your man of God that he is able to remain strong and chaste in the face of flagrant sexual temptations. With sex as freely available as it is nowadays, few men are able to stay pure unless somebody is praying. Certainly, one of those praying better be him, but at least one other person who is praying for him in this regard ought to be you.

Becoming Maximum Marriage Material

The second element of your marriage prayers should be prayer for yourself. Pray that God will be molding you into the perfect partner for your future mate. Remember, you want Him to form in you those characteristics that will make you a maximum marriage partner for your spouse-to-be.

Another area of prayer that you dare not neglect is that of committing your mate to God in prayer. Consciously and willfully, you must give that person back to the Lord.

Place your partner in God's hands now, even if you and your spouse have not yet met. Acknowledge Jesus as Lord of your relationship *before* you meet Mr. or Miss Right, and there will be much less chance of priority problems when you and your spouse finally get together. Make your relationship a *threesome* while there are only two of you.

When the third party arrives, he will not be an intruder; he (or she) will be someone for whom you have prayed. You may be pleasantly surprised to find that you feel like you have known this person for a long time, because you have prayed for him so faithfully.

What's It All About? While you are yet single, you should also pray that God will grant you a clear vision of what marriage is all about. God's pattern for matrimony was laid out in the Garden of Eden, from the beginning of time. All three ingredients—leaving, cleaving, and the becoming one are essential in a biblically based marriage (Genesis 2:24).

Leaving. In order for a Christian marriage to take place, the bride and groom must "leave" Mom and Dad, and strike out on their own. This does not mean that the new couple never see their parents again, never call, never write or visit their families once the wedding is over. It does mean that you and your mate are beginning a new family; the cords that tie you to your parents must be thoroughly cut. Your wedding is an announcement to the world that you will no longer be depending upon Mom and Dad for protection, security, money, food, clothing, or housing. From this day forward, you will be working together with your husband or wife to meet your own needs. Certainly, loving parental assistance or advice should never be ignored or rudely rejected, but if a couple is to make it in marriage, they must make it on their own.

For this reason, most counselors frown upon newlyweds living in the home of the parents. If you are not ready to start your own household, you are probably not ready for marriage. Too much parental intervention in the lives of married children, even when given out of loving hearts, can only bring havoc.

Once you say "I do," you are no longer "Dad's boy" or "Mommy's little girl." Man, you belong to your wife; you are her husband. Woman, you belong to your husband; you are his wife. With a few puffs of air from your lungs, your entire list of priorities has changed.

Cleaving. As you leave the parent-child relationship for a Christian marriage, you are to "cleave" together, permanently united with your partner. The word *cleave* carries the connotation of inseparability. Indeed, hardly anything on earth can separate a husband and wife who are cleaving together.

Clearly, in God's original design, He did not intend divorce to be an option. The word *cleave* has the meaning of "to glue, to cling." The marriage of two people can be likened to the pasting together of two individual pieces of paper. Once they have been united, it is almost impossible to separate them without tearing or otherwise severely damaging one or both of the individual parts. This is a concept that flies in the face of modern society; yet God's ideas on marriage have not changed.

Becoming One Flesh. It is only as a couple leave their parents and cleave to each other that they can truly become "one flesh." Surely, the idea of becoming one has sexual implications. Intercourse ought to be the ultimate expression of unity in the marriage of two people who are totally committed to Christ and to each other. Sex should be a spiritual experience, as well as physical.

Nevertheless, becoming one flesh involves more than the sexual; it means to mold together two personalities into a perfect, harmonious unity. This takes lots of time and lots of unconditional love. It does not magically occur on your wedding day (or your wedding night!). Becoming one person is a process that will begin, to some extent, even before your wedding day, and will continue throughout your marriage.

Note, though, *oneness* does not mean *sameness*. Becoming one person does not erase each other's personality. Marriage is not the subversion or suppression of your personalities; it is a willful merger of lives, a mutual acceptance of each other as he or she is. It is a thorough blending of persons wherein the two become so intertwined that their individuality, though not obliterated, is overshadowed by their inseparable oneness.

These are things that need to be thoroughly prayed through before you bite into the marriage apple. If you are going to partake of it, be sure that you have prayed over it, that you are as fully prepared as possible for what you will find inside. Always keep in mind: don't bite the apple 'til you check for worms!

Epilogue

The moment I saw her walk through the doors of the church, I knew my single days were numbered. She was a picture of biblical femininity, her outward, dark-haired beauty enhanced by a radiance that seemed to emanate from within.

"Hello!" she called enthusiastically. "Are you Ken Abraham?"

"Yes, I am," I answered, surprised that she knew my name.

"Hi! My name is Angela, and I'm going to Hawaii with you and the other Watchmen on one of your tour groups." She introduced some other girls, who were also going to Hawaii with us.

"Oh, really?" I nearly whooped with delight. "That's great!"

We talked for the next few minutes, and, all too soon, it was time for the service to begin.

"Hey, I'll see you later, after the program!" I called to the girls, as they started toward the sanctuary. Angela smiled in return, and I thought I was in heaven.

Later, at the home of some mutual friends, Angela and I had a chance to get acquainted. We had many things in common. She had become a Christian at an early age and had been raised in a home and church environment very similar to my own. Her vivacious personality was contagious, and we were soon discussing everything from music to politics, as if we were two long-lost friends just finding each other.

Over the next few months, Angela and I communicated mostly by mail. She lived in Michigan and I in Pennsylvania, so dating was next to impossible. Fortunately for us, in less than three months following our introduction, the Watchmen were back in Michigan on a concert tour. At that early juncture in our relationship, Angela and I agreed to begin praying about a possible future together. We hadn't even been out on a date yet!

Three months passed before I saw her again. Meanwhile, our phone and postage bills were skyrocketing. The distance that separated us was an unexpected blessing. It caused us to recognize immediately that our relationship could not be based upon physical expressions; we needed a much firmer foundation than sweet nothings, hugs, and kisses. We knew that if we were to have a future together, we had to be able to communicate clearly and honestly. We had to establish a trust in each other. We were convinced that our relationship had to be built upon Jesus Christ.

Angela and I put into practice the principles that I have shared in this book. In our early courtship, for example, we spent most of our time talking, getting to know each other better. Certainly we enjoyed going places, doing fun things, and expressing our affection, but time together was short, and there was so much to share with each other.

We didn't fall in love. In fact, you might say we slipped into love through the back door! Before we met, Angela and I were insistent that singleness was our permanent lot. We had grown so ingrained in single living that both of us were reluctant to admit we were vulnerable to love's darts. When the Lord brought us together, He began to change those attitudes, though He received little help from us.

We spent the next two years seeking God's will concerning our relationship. Why so long? It took two years for the Lord to teach us the many things we needed to know before getting married. Some of us are slow learners!

Was it difficult to be patient and wait upon God? You bet it was! Was it worth the wait? Without a doubt!

What about sexual tensions during this time? Did we have those pressures, too? You know we did! The longer our relationship ran, the more we wanted to express our feelings physically as well as verbally. However, we knew that our heavenly Father could not bless our future if we chose to ignore His firm commands regarding our sexuality.

How did we know we were right for each other? Well, first of all we prayed. Every time we talked by phone, we prayed. Every time we were together, we prayed. We prayed individually; we prayed as a couple. Then, we allowed the Lord enough time to answer our prayers and show us His will.

As mentioned earlier, we had a lot of factors going for us, including the approval of family and friends. Although all our common interests and concerns were important contributors, none of these was the primary reason we decided to get married.

Angela and I chose to join our lives together because we were confident that we would count more for Christ as a couple than we could as unmarried individuals. The numbers were right. One plus one equaled more than two!